HOW TO BECOME A

CREATIVE PERSON

T0159935

IRH Press

BOOKS
IRH PRESS
New York

ISBN 13: 978-1-942125-84-6
ISBN 10: 1-942125-84-4
Cover Image: lovelyday12/shutterstock.com

Printed in Canada

First Edition

HOW TO
BECOME A
CREATIVE
PERSON

RYUHO OKAWA

IRH Press

Contents

CHAPTER ONE

How to Become a Creative Person

Creative Power that Comes from Imagination

Preface

Many of the spiritual truths I see as a matter of course may be surprising to my new readers.

I believe work productivity is based on the law of cause and effect, but it is difficult to explain in words the importance of the process of producing positive results. For example, reading more than 2,000 books a year does not necessarily allow you to write as many books as you want. Rather, the more books you read, the more confusing and difficult it becomes for you to organize your thoughts. This is probably true for over 90 percent of people. Those who become too immersed in miscellaneous information during youth will grow up to be well-versed only in trivia or the kind of information found in tabloids.

You need talent, heavenly blessings, and perseverance to cultivate your abilities to differentiate the main issue from unimportant details and to grasp the essence. You must always strive to find gold in the sand and keep on polishing the rough diamond.

Ryuho Okawa
Master & CEO of Happy Science Group
May 16, 2018

CHAPTER ONE

How to Become a Creative Person

Creative Power that Comes from Imagination

Lecture given on August 27, 2011,
at Sohonzan Nasu Shoja of Happy Science,
Tochigi Prefecture, Japan

1

The Habit to Gain Better Ideas

Are your ideas truly new and original?

The word "creative" in the chapter title "How to Become a Creative Person" means the ability to create something new. In this world, there are many things that have already been created and many people who have come up with something new. If you work hard to research and develop something without knowing it already exists or someone else has already discovered it, the years or decades you spent on research and development can go to waste.

To become a creative person in modern civilization, you cannot invent everything yourself, like Robinson Crusoe who lived alone on a remote island. With so many people in this world, there is usually someone else who has already thought of the same ideas you have.

Save time to create something new

I once watched a Japanese TV program called *Cambria Palace* featuring a conversation between Toru Kenjo, president of publisher Gentosha Inc., and Susumu Fujita, president of CyberAgent, Inc. At that time, Mr. Fujita was only about 38 years old. He is one of the presidents who have survived in the IT industry, where many companies go under due to severe competition. His company went public when he was 26, and he developed it until it had about 2,000 employees by the time he was in his 30s.

In the program, Mr. Fujita said something along the lines of, "Even if you think no one would ever think of ideas as original as yours, there are at least three people who have the same ideas as you. Quite a few people come to similar conclusions and ideas as a result of thinking hard and pursuing something."

Even in new businesses, it is not possible for one person at the top to always come up with new ideas. If you can quickly learn what others have already researched, found, or created, you can save time by using their ideas. In other words, there is no need for you to redo what others have already done all over again. Take pi, which equals "3.14...," for example. You can certainly recalculate this yourself now, but it would be a waste of time to do so because a considerable number of digits of pi have already been calculated by computers.

You could end up wasting your time pursuing something if you do not know it has already been achieved. This applies to your studies as well as your work. In case something of quality has already been made, you first need to study it and learn from it. Then, you can consider whether there is anything you can add to improve it.

Do not solely rely on inspiration

It is too naive to think inspiration will come to you from heaven if you simply sit back and wait. As a religion, we at Happy Science greatly value revelations and inspiration from heaven, and we know such forces are truly at work. But it is important to integrate the powers of inspiration with daily diligent efforts. When someone who does not habitually make diligent efforts says, "I have come up with something no one else has ever thought of. This is a new invention," oftentimes, his or her ideas are not new or original.

But there are, of course, times when you do come up with something completely new. Once you start thinking of one idea, new ideas will emerge one after another. With training or with accumulated effort, it will become increasingly easier to think of better ideas.

2

When Imagination Turns into Creative Power

What does it mean to be "imaginative"?

This chapter is titled "How to Become a Creative Person," but before becoming a creative person, you must first be someone with imagination. Imagination is the ability to envision something or to think of something in your mind. Having imagination is essential because it will help you become creative; you will turn from being imaginative to being creative. So it is very important to expand the "imaginative space" within your mind.

Let me give you an example. We currently have Head Temple Nasu Shoja and Happy Science Academy junior and senior high schools in Nasu in Tochigi Prefecture. I bought the land more than 10 years ago (at the time of the lecture). Actually, this land was a golf course that had gone out of business. The previous landowner had invested ¥15 billion (about US$137 million) during the golf course development boom in the 1980s to develop this golf course. But by the time it was completed, the boom had passed and the course was closed without being used even once. Since then, the land was left unused for about 10 years, and the landowner was troubled and was looking for a buyer. He wanted to somehow sell it because it had cost him ¥50 million (about US$455,000) a year just to mow the grass and to maintain it.

When I went to the site, I looked at the landscape and asked myself, "How can I make use of this land?" First, the idea of building a shoja (temple) came to mind. After giving it another thought for a while, I came up with the idea of using it for a school. As I walked around the largest pond on the property, I thought it would be nice to have a large golden stupa around the pond and imagined that the reflection of the stupa in the pond would look really beautiful. In this way, I imagined various facilities being built as I looked around the empty space.

This is the power of imagination. This will become the power to create the future. The essential thing is what you visualize in your mind—in other words, it is whether you can imagine people doing various activities there or something new being created there.

Use your imagination to eliminate excuses one by one

On hearing my ideas, the management executives of Happy Science at the time expressed many reasons why it was not possible to build a school there. But I did not listen to any of them. If you think something is impossible, then it will of course be impossible. Effort is what makes it possible. I, myself, was able to clearly "see" a school being built there and the students studying and participating in club activities. And because I imagined the school being built there and was determined to build it, we managed to build it in the end.

The place where the Happy Science Academy stands now was originally developed for a golf course, so the land sloped up and down and had many hills, valleys, and ponds to make golf more exciting. Because of this, the executives assumed that the land was not suitable for a school and were only looking for a vast, flat land. But I told them that simply leveling the land will solve the problem and had it done.

Before that, the executives made many excuses why a school cannot be built there. For example, they said, "If the students played baseball here, all the balls they hit would roll down the slope and become home runs. The balls may even roll away and fall into a hollow, and the students may never get them back. Is that okay? If we can't create a proper field, the students won't be able to play baseball." I heard many reasons like this on why a school cannot be built there. So I told them to level the land by moving the soil from the hill to the low areas. In this way, whether or not you have imagination is essential to become a creative person.

There was also the issue of implementing a boarding school system at Happy Science Academy. There were many difficult concerns, such as whether parents would be willing to let their daughters out of their homes to live in the dormitories or whether junior high school students, unlike high school students, would feel too lonely if they lived in dormitories. But in the end we managed to establish a boarding school.

Ultimately, it all comes down to your imagination. First, you need to use your imagination and visualize what you want to make happen. If you can "see" yourself making it happen, then put it into practice and actually accomplish it. This will become your creative power or the power to create things.

3
How Highly Creative People Generate Ideas

What we can learn from the story of Columbus' egg

The ability to create an "idea" in your mind is very important. This may be what was regarded as "magic" in ancient times. Regardless of what the idea is, it is very difficult to be the first one to come up with an idea, as illustrated by the story of Columbus' egg.

Columbus sailed westward toward India and discovered a land. At a party celebrating the discovery, Columbus was told, "Anyone can do what you did." So he asked the attendants of the party, "Is there anyone who can make an egg stand on its end on this table?" Seeing no one could do it, he said, "This is how you make it stand," and crushed the end of the egg to make it stand.

Not many people can come up with the idea of crushing the end of an egg to make it stand. It is not possible to make an egg stand as it is because it rolls over very easily, but if you can come up with the idea of crushing one of its ends, you can make it stand. Once someone has done it, anyone will be able to do it, but coming up with such an idea for the very first time is difficult. This is the story of Columbus' egg.

New business opportunities lie in familiar foods as well

There are plenty of other stories like this. For example, nowadays, sliced bread is commonly sold in shops in town, but originally bread was sold in loaves. One day, someone came up with the idea of cutting the bread into thin slices to make it easier for people to eat it, and it sold very well.

There is a similar story regarding sugar. Sugar naturally absorbs water from the air and hardens if left exposed. This quality was considered to be a drawback and a problem with sugar because granulated sugar was considered better for coffee or tea. However, there was a person who thought, "Why not harden it from the start?" This was the beginning of sugar cubes. The inventor of sugar cubes—sugar in block shape—made a great fortune with just that idea.

It is natural for sugar to harden once it absorbs water, but the person "thought in reverse" and wondered what would happen if sugar was hardened from the start. If you harden it into sugar cubes, it would certainly be more convenient when you sell them in packs or carry them around. Furthermore, there is something elegant about putting sugar cubes in your coffee or tea, and it is not bad. But no one had ever come up with the idea of sugar cubes until then because people generally thought sugar should be kept dry; they thought it would take too much time for sugar to melt once it hardens. The person who came up with the idea of sugar cubes made a lot of money with such a simple idea. Things like this can happen.

In this way, you can create something new in this world depending on your way of thinking. You can find new business opportunities or seeds of new businesses there.

Train yourself to think creatively

Some examples of highly creative professions that require a variety of new ideas are writing and art. Corporate managers—especially new business owners—also do highly creative work. The same is true for inventors who create something that did not exist before. These people are not only highly creative but also do not neglect the basic efforts that are necessary.

In addition to basic efforts, it is important to think about various things from different angles. By trying different approaches—for example, flipping something over, making it bigger or smaller, or turning it upside down—you can sometimes get unexpected results. People who train themselves to think creatively in this way will be able to take on many new challenges.

4

Recognize Your Strengths

*There is no need to let go of
your unique dispositions or characteristics*

When you try to create something new, do not be afraid of failing. You cannot know how things will turn out until you actually try them. It is important to think about what people do not normally think about.

For example, it is generally said that only 30–40 percent of early promotions are successful, but when you actually appoint a young and inexperienced person to a higher position, oftentimes you will unexpectedly find the person to be highly capable. In some cases, those who are regarded as arrogant often do very well, which is shocking.

To give an example from Happy Science, one of the young secretaries who accompanied me to my events always looked bored. He lacked courtesy and had a sulky attitude, as if to say, "This job isn't interesting. I can do the work of a much bigger scale." So I said, "He's such an arrogant secretary. Let's make him the director general." He was then assigned to the director general position of a division, and, to my surprise, he did good work as the director general. Later, that person was promoted to the executive director position (at the time of the lecture). In this way, sometimes you find unexpected personnel to be surprisingly capable.

Of course, you should be able to do what others can do, but you do not need to let go of your unique disposition or characteristics. Young people tend to be misunderstood, but they actually have the right to be misunderstood. Your unique qualities can often represent your strong points, so do not overlook them. It is not good to regard them as your weaknesses and dwell on them too much.

Feel nothing toward jealous attacks

Smart people tend to have a sharp tongue and talk bluntly, so they are sometimes disliked by others. For example, when such people work in the sales department and start to make their mark, they are often bullied by their seniors or superiors. But once they achieve more outstanding results, these harassments will stop because workers are usually assessed by "numbers" in such departments. Until then, they often suffer from relationship issues.

If you are bullied for your bad character and bad attitude, you cannot make any excuses, but if you are bullied for your successes and contribution to the company, you must stand firm against bullying. Bullying in this case is nothing but jealousy. Unless you dodge these "bullets of jealousy," you can never get ahead.

What jealous people dislike the most is to meet someone who is not afraid of being the target of jealousy. Contrarily, it is easy for them to deal with someone who withdraws as soon as he or she is targeted; their jealousy would be paid off if the targeted person quickly retracts his or her head like a turtle at the bullets of their jealousy. In this case, they can happily get along with the person on equal footing.

However, it is difficult to deal with people who do not care about being envied no matter how intensely they are being targeted. The jealous person will eventually start to feel bad about feeling jealous and come to think twice and wonder, "If I have time to feel jealous of others, maybe I should try harder instead." So feeling nothing toward jealous attacks can also have a positive effect on society.

People who have distinguished characteristics that stick out like "horns" may have many worries about relationship issues or their character when they are young. They may experience many struggles, but contrary to their expectation, their negative self-image is often surprisingly inaccurate. This is worth noting.

5

Subconscious Mind Manifesting in Romantic Relationships

Your subconscious mind could be seeking someone who rejects you

In romantic relationships, young men are often attracted to women who will give them the opposite result of what they want. This is not just someone else's problem; in fact, I also had this tendency.

Young men who are aiming at lofty goals or are aspiring to accomplish something big in the future are more likely to be rejected by women, so please be careful. Perhaps it is misleading to say that they are "more likely to be rejected"; to put it another way, these men tend to fall in love with a woman they could never have a successful relationship or marriage with.

This is because they are subconsciously looking for someone who would reject them. They approach women who are out of their league and are unreachable. They do this because they want to improve themselves. In other words, in their hearts they think, "I can't stay like this. I want to develop myself more."

How can they keep improving themselves eternally? To do so, all they need is an "eternal woman" who is forever unattainable. In reality, there is no such person as an "eternal woman," but the woman who always refuses them could become "the eternal one" for them, and that is why they tend to choose someone who is most likely to refuse them.

If they dare to approach such a person, they will be rejected, disappointed, and heartbroken. They may end up "going into hiding" and take years or even a decade to resurface. During that time, they will work hard while putting themselves down by saying, "I'm no good. I'm not good enough."

Young men who aspire to improve themselves tend to go through this process unconsciously, so they need to be careful. They should not think they are no good because of a broken heart. Oftentimes, they unconsciously choose a partner who is likely to reject them because they want to develop themselves. I know that highly talented men in particular have this tendency.

The true nature of attractive but cunning women

The subconscious mind can manifest in romantic relationships for women as well. Some women are attractive but a little cunning. This is the first time I am talking about this type of women. They are an extremely tantalizing existence for men. Such a woman is attractive but when men approach her, they will first get short shrift, so they will assume she does not like them. But after a short while, she will suddenly act as if she likes them, so men are tossed about and toyed with. There are such women, but young men cannot understand their nature. They find these women mysterious and do not know how to view them.

However, their true nature is surprisingly simple to explain. In fact, these attractive but cunning women are extremely proud of themselves but also have a very strong sense of inferiority. They have excessive self-respect and pride but they also have a huge sense of inferiority, and these two feelings are intertwined inside them. Because these feelings alternate as they emerge, the woman treats the man who approaches her in a similar way as how a cat plays with a mouse and confuses him.

These women are well aware that they have such a tendency, but because they do not know how to overcome it, they unconsciously end up treating men in this way. Women who have this tendency need to know that they act in such ways because they are overly confident and, at the same time, have a deep-rooted inferiority complex. If they themselves can clearly understand this nature, they will be able to express themselves more naturally.

The secret to success in a romantic relationship

If you can express yourself naturally, as if to say, "This is who I am," you will rarely be misunderstood. One of the secrets to succeeding in romantic relationships is to be able to understand the other person. So strive to understand each other.

You cannot truly be happy in a relationship if you misunderstand one another or do not understand each other. To break through and overcome this problem, you need to come up with a new perspective. This is another aspect of creativity.

6

The Mechanism to Turn Your Thoughts into Reality

The moment when answers suddenly come to you

The best of creativity comes to those in creative work, such as writers and novelists, and to those who launch new businesses. I also write many books and plan and develop a variety of projects, so I am actually "creativity" itself. I have come up with over 10,000 ideas to date, and these ideas have made Happy Science what it is today.

The key to producing ideas is to keep thinking day after day. Even if you are doing something else, you have to continue thinking about an issue and keep it in the back of your mind at all times. You never know when the answer will come to you, so always be aware of your problem.

If you are aware of your problem, the answer to the problem will suddenly come to you when you are working hard on something, which may not necessarily be related to the problem you want to solve. I have experienced this many times.

The amazing benefits of meditation and prayer

Happy Science believers, in particular, regularly practice meditation and prayer. They know meditation and prayer truly have power. This is one of the strengths of Happy Science believers.

Even for me, mastering the secrets of the power of the mind in my 20s had a great impact on my life. It was greatly significant for me to have discovered, realized, and grasped the truth that what I clearly picture in my mind and decide to make come true will truly come to pass in real life. Usually, people cannot realize their ideas because they fail to fix the ideas in their minds and hold on to them firmly.

I now make various spiritual phenomena happen, such as receiving messages from spirits. I can generally summon any spirit in a matter of seconds. This means my thoughts and voice reach anywhere on Earth, including the spirit world; the ones who are called upon receive my thoughts. This is how things work in the world of thoughts.

If you strongly keep wishing to accomplish something, be it starting a business or realizing an idea, it means you are constantly sending out such thoughts. There is always someone "catching" your thoughts, and that person will show up as your business partner or supporter. Or if you do artistic work, someone will appear and help you with your work.

Meditate to gain ideas and
pray to gain supporters

In the world of the mind, thoughts are instantly transmitted to the other person. I have demonstrated this truth through various phenomena. This is what is truly happening when you practice meditation and prayer.

Meditation is more about receiving others' thoughts; meditation allows you to receive the thoughts of various people around the world and thoughts of spiritual beings with whom you have a special connection. In the case of Happy Science believers, they may receive guidance from the guiding spirit group of Happy Science. Meditation is quite a passive practice, but this is also an important way to gain ideas.

Prayer, on the other hand, is an active practice; you are the one sending out the thoughts. In the same way as I conduct spiritual phenomena, your prayers will also travel around the world in a matter of seconds. Information on the Internet is not the only thing that spreads around the world—thoughts are also circulating around the world.

The thoughts I send out from Japan will reach anywhere, be it America, Australia, Africa, and Europe. Although I do not know who is catching them or where the person is, the thoughts I send out will surely reach someone. After a while, that person will appear and start to participate in our activities and become our supporter. If you are determined to make something happen, it will eventually be realized.

7

Master the Power of the Mind

How to use the power of meditation and prayer

The power to make your wishes come true is the same as the magic that has existed since ancient times. Magic can be either white magic or black magic depending on how it is used—for good or for evil. I want things to improve as much as possible, and I hope you will use the power of your mind for a good purpose.

It would be a problem to focus your mind on crime, for example, and think, "How can I break the safe over there?" and to use meditation to commit crime. You would be no different from Lupin III.[1] Someone who wants to be a great thief may wonder, "How can I break into that one-meter-thick iron safe? Should I dig from underground?" and meditate on the way to break into the safe, but this is not the right way to use meditation. Instead of breaking into safes to steal money, I want people to engage in proper and legitimate work or business to earn millions or tens of millions of dollars.

You can achieve many things by using the power of your mind in the right direction and practicing meditation and prayer. You will understand this to be true more and more as time passes.

The way successful people use the power of their minds in society

Thoughts are a real power, indeed. Meditation is also a power and so is prayer. Imagination, or visualization, is a real power, too.

These are all abilities school exams cannot measure. What is measured by school exams is the rough extent of your abilities; you can see this for yourself from your exam scores. But once you go out in society, you will see an outcome different from the exam results because the power of the mind, which cannot be measured by school exams, will come into play. People who were completely in the shadows of other high achievers at school may attain success. These people know how to use the power of the mind.

If you visualize the accumulation of wealth in your mind and wish to build wealth, you will eventually be given the work to achieve it. Similarly, those who strongly wish to expand their relationships will see it truly happening in reality.

Mastering the power of the mind is, in fact, the road to enlightenment, and this road is open for anyone to follow—within the scope of what they are allowed to achieve. But if you are ignorant of the power of the mind, you will not be able to do so.

This is not only true in the world of Harry Potter. When Harry Potter, the main character, waves his little wand, what he thinks in his mind manifests and comes true. But we do not actually need a wand like that. We can achieve many things *only* with the power of the mind.

I have witnessed this, too. I have been saying, "We'll make Happy Science a world religion," "We will spread Buddha's Truth throughout the world," and "Spread this Truth to the end of the world," and we are slowly getting closer to achieving these goals. The teachings of Happy Science have now spread to over 100 countries (164 countries as of August 2021), and it will soon spread to 200 countries. I believe the day we go to the "end of the world" and spread the Truth to the penguins is nearing [*laughs*].

Young people have the potential to become creative people

To create something, first, it is important to produce an idea and then believe in the power of your mind. In doing so, youth is never a hindrance because the purer your wishes are, the more likely it is for these wishes to come true. Rather, being young means you have great potential.

So do not put a limit on your abilities or worry about feeling inferior. Know that thoughts come true.

Nevertheless, even if you have understood the power of the mind, please do not deny the achievements you and others have made through earthly efforts in various things, such as school studies or club activities. The efforts you and others have taken at a given point in time are good, so please evaluate and accept them objectively. I just want you to know that you can make up for what you lack and make further advancements using the powers that are beyond this world.

TRANSLATOR'S NOTE

1 Lupin III is a fictional gentleman thief from a Japanese manga series.

Quietly Persevere

Even if you hope for something,
It often does not come true.
Even if you wish for something,
You may fail and get hurt.
As a result of experiencing such setbacks,
Many people forget to hold on to their aspirations.
Perhaps this is true for 99 people out of 100.
Some people even abandon their faith
Just because their wishes do not come true.
It is very sad.

These people had once arrived at the gate.
But being unable to pass through it,
They turned back.
It means they have failed to keep their faith.

Young people experience many failures and setbacks
Simply because there is too much they do not know—
They do not have enough knowledge and experience.
It does not mean
The laws to make wishes come true
Or faith is wrong.
Nothing can be achieved if you quit after three days.

To realize your deepest wishes,
Whether in study, sports, or work,
You must quietly persevere.

First, give it three years.
Then 10 years.
And continue to work hard for 20 years, then 30 years.
By then,
You will be standing firmly on the land of your ideals.

CHAPTER TWO

Power Up Your Intellectual Strength

The Art of Reading to Triumph in Life

Lecture given on August 26, 2010,
at Chiba Shoshinkan of Happy Science,
Chiba Prefecture, Japan

1

Overcome the Intellectual Inferiority Complex

The meaning of the chapter title

The literal translation of the original Japanese title for this lecture is "How to Build Up Your Intellectual Physical Strength." This was not the title I chose, but it was given to me after we collected requests for the kinds of lectures young people would like to hear.

It is a rather complicated title. If the title was "how to build up your intellect" or "how to build up your physical strength," it would be easy to understand, but what is "building up the intellectual physical strength"? It is like a Zen *koan*; perhaps we could hold a one-hour seminar just to contemplate the meaning of this phrase.

I, too, have thought about the meaning of this phrase and determined it would be "Power Up Your Intellectual Strength" in English. Simply put, it would be "how to enhance your intellectual strength further." Sometimes it is surprisingly easy to get the meaning of a difficult Japanese phrase if you try to translate it to English.

Young people tend to worry about being unintelligent

When we surveyed young people—especially university students in Japan—on the questions they would like to have answered, we found that they were particularly interested in intellectual pursuits or how to study. For example, they wanted to know how to pick out the important points when studying, how to identify the key 20 percent of the information based on the 80/20 rule,[1] or how to develop the power of concentration. Nowadays, the expression "training one's brainpower" is often used. So people may imagine enhancing one's intellectual ability as being the same as training one's brainpower.

Many people around the age of entering college probably compare their abilities with those of their classmates or students who are one or two years senior or junior to them and think, "I'm surprised there are such smart, genius-type people out in the world. In contrast, this head of mine works as slow as a camel walks." This is my honest impression. They may feel like saying, "Come on, horse, run faster!" or "What can I do about this head of mine that is ready to go into summer vacation at any moment?"

In fact, I, myself, felt that way, too. I was exactly the same as everyone else and used to think, "Can't I do something about my head? Would I be a little smarter if I hit the back of my head with a hammer?" Because I am originally from Shikoku Island, my peers who had grown up in Tokyo and had graduated from elite high schools appeared very smart and intelligent to me. I worried that someone like me who had crawled out from the countryside was not born very smart.

I remember being seized by anxiety and worrying, "I worked hard and managed to crawl up like a mud turtle to enter the University of Tokyo, but maybe I am in the wrong place. Maybe I am out of place for studying and listening to the classes in this national university. Perhaps I'm wasting national tax money by studying here." I had the feeling that other students were a little more efficient in their studies and knew everything they had to know.

The reality of geniuses and brilliant people

Since then, I went through various experiences and realized there are no such people as "stunning geniuses" in the world. When people call someone a "genius," it is often due to some misunderstanding; they do not actually know the person well, and in many cases, they only see one side of him or her.

When I examined the lifestyles, studies, and personal histories of those who were referred to as "geniuses," I found that there are reasons for them to be called by such a title. And I came to understand there is not much of a difference in people's natural abilities.

I saw many people who excelled in their studies but quickly forgot everything they had studied once the exam was over. I was shocked to see the true nature of such "geniuses." It was unbelievable to see that everything they had learned was truly "gone" as soon as the exam was over. There were many such people who only remembered things for the day of the exam. You would not study in that way if you truly love learning or love academics. Those who quickly forget what they learned after the exam probably see studies as a mere stepping-stone.

This made me realize I was actually true to myself when studying, although my academic progress was slow. As I studied, I would always make sure I was developing my abilities.

The only way to outdo geniuses

The first realization I gained around the age of 20 was this: "There is only one way to outdo people who are smarter than you." There may be some difference in intelligence due to our parents. A child born from excellent parents and a child born from mediocre parents may happen to be studying at the same school, and their abilities may well be different from the start. Even so, there is still a way—the only way—to win. It is to read more books than other people. I found this to be the way to outdo others.

After all, once you accumulate a certain amount of knowledge, there is a point at which others can no longer catch up to you. Once you reach this irreversible point, other people can no longer surpass you. If the difference in the amount of knowledge is not very big, the smarter person may appear sharper than the other person, but once the difference in knowledge or studies exceeds a certain level, the gap in intelligence will become irreversible. I came to understand there is such a point.

In the field of science, such as math or physics, there may be other necessary factors, rather than just the mere amount of knowledge, to reach that point and surpass others. But in the fields of general education and the studies of arts and humanities, having about a ten-year gap in the amount of knowledge will make it impossible for others to surpass your ability. I discovered this from my own experience.

So, if you think you are not smart enough, it is essential to read books. In the beginning, you may feel a sense of inferiority, but as you read more books and gain more knowledge, that feeling will gradually fade. Before you realize it, you will find yourself being absorbed in the study itself, even though you may previously have been fretting over how inferior you were in competition with others.

In fact, this is nothing but a battle against yourself; you are not fighting against others but against yourself. The question is how much you will demand from yourself in deepening your study or how much you will pursue your studies. This endeavor will work to develop your abilities.

2

How to Turn a Mediocre Person into a Wise Person

The merit of deciding what to give up and narrow down

People tend to admire all-round geniuses such as Leonardo da Vinci, but in reality, there is almost no one who is an all-round genius.

It may seem like I am doing many things simultaneously, but I actually am not. In fact, I accomplish each task as if I am stacking bricks or blocks one by one. Once I lay the groundwork for a task and expand it, I move on to another task to lay the groundwork for that. I build upon my work in this way. Because I formulate and complete my tasks relatively quickly, this makes it look as though I am doing many things simultaneously. So in reality, we cannot do many things all at once; we can only accomplish one task at a time.

What matters is to decide how much time you are going to spend on learning something and to what extent you are going to explore it. Even if you tackle several things at the same time, it is almost impossible to master them all. It is important to be aware of this. Those who learn to identify the things to give up at a young age will become wise, whereas those who do not will become unwise.

People who overestimate their abilities will try to do everything they take an interest in and tackle various things at the same time, only to end up not mastering anything at all. On the other hand, some people realize and tell themselves, "I'm not particularly smart. I know from my past achievements and the evaluations of the people around me that I am far from being a genius. With such ordinary abilities, I have to narrow down what I do, focus on a certain field, and master it." These people are likely to achieve better results and enter the road to success.

How to master four different fields of study in one year

In fact, everyone has the same amount of time in a day, and there is not much of a difference in people's abilities.

So, if you try to do several things at the same time, your energy will become dispersed and you often end up failing to accomplish anything.

Even if you set a goal of mastering four different fields of study to a certain level in one year, it is difficult to tackle all of them simultaneously. So, in this case, you have to spend about three months on each subject and master them one by one. Once you study a subject to a certain level, you can get an overall sense of the subject.

Suppose you think, "I'm not good at economics, but I want to be able to talk about it with other people." In this case, you need to concentrate on reading and studying books and articles on economics for three months—or six months depending on the person—to gain a certain level of understanding. Then you will be able to understand the overall picture of economics.

Once you solidify your knowledge on a field to a certain degree and have reached a level where you feel you will no longer regress, you can move on to another field of study. For example, if you think the knowledge of economics alone is not enough and want to study politics as well, you can then concentrate on studying politics.

When studying, it is essential to build the foundation in one area of study to a certain extent before moving on to the next area, as if you are stacking blocks. If you try to tackle many subjects at the same time, your understanding will remain fuzzy in all fields, and your studies will often end up being incomplete.

You need to be stoic to master a language

The same is true for learning languages. In general, the number of languages people can perfectly master is two or three at most. Even those with a high level of language-learning aptitude can only master up to four or five languages. Some people claim they have mastered more than five languages, but in most cases, they have only studied them to the extent of a hobby and often do not have high proficiency. In reality, it is difficult to master so many languages.

It is of course good to be able to use several languages, but mastering English as a second language alone is not so easy. If you want to master English as a second language, you have to be stoic and give up on learning other languages after a certain level. Should you decide to study another language simultaneously, you need to aim to reach a conversational level only and focus first on studying English until you have a good command of English. If you try to simultaneously learn several languages at equally high levels, in many cases, you only end up spending a tremendous amount of time studying them and fail to master any of them.

In the end, people who realize the limit of their abilities and narrow down their focus will accomplish a lot in study or work, as if they have boundless abilities. In contrast, those who believe they can do everything will be unable to accomplish anything at all. This is worth noting.

A tip for studying a variety of fields

I now have a wide range of knowledge and understanding of a variety of fields because I have studied various matters that drew my interest. But honestly speaking, I have had to more or less focus on one field at a time to reach the level of "mastery."

When doing so, I would adjust the extent of my focus. Because you have other subjects to study as well, you simply cannot concentrate on one field and disregard the others. So it is important to adjust the extent of your focus on the different subjects.

3

Discover Your Aptitude and Talent

You cannot tell what major you are suited for until you actually study it

There is also the issue of your likes and dislikes or your aptitude or talent for a certain specialization. This is inevitable.

People choose their major upon entering university. Some may select their major based on the level of their academic ability, whereas others may do so based on how advantageous it is when finding employment. But in reality, there are people who are suited and unsuited for their majors. In fact, it is often difficult to know in advance what major you are suited for, and you usually cannot tell until you actually study it.

For example, there are students in medical schools who faint at the sight of blood. These students probably chose to enroll in medical school simply because it was a top-level school or because doctors can make a lot of money. Apparently, about one-third of the students in medical schools say they almost fainted when observing a dissection. But to be blunt, such people are not suited to be doctors and should not have chosen to go to medical school in the first place. They probably enrolled in medical school because they had high enough academic abilities to pass the exams, but they should not have chosen that path unless they were fond of dissections or were the type of people who could become fishmongers filleting fish.

Goethe was not suited to study law

Taking an old example, there was a great German writer named Goethe (1749–1832). He was a poet and an artist, but he had actually enrolled in law school and studied law in college. However, "fortunately," he was not very good at studying law, contrary to his parents' expectations. Studying law was not interesting to him at all, and he would struggle to absorb any information about it. So he began to study literature, art, and other miscellaneous subjects outside of law and became more knowledgeable that way. As a result, those endeavors came to fruition later on.

He did not have much talent in law, but in his case, this turned out to be good. If he had done well in law school, his sensibilities would most likely have died away. In that sense, Goethe may have been "given up" by academics rather than him "giving up" on them. Even if the field of study you happen to choose was not suited for you, it does not necessarily mean you are not smart. No one would say Goethe was unintelligent now; rather, he is actually one of the greatest geniuses in Germany. He simply was not academically cut out for law. I am not sure whether he had given up on the study of law or law had given up on him, but his inabilities in that field luckily led him to pursue his side interests. Sometimes, the job you do on the side for pleasure can fortunately bear fruit in this way.

The impression of the novels by Yukio Mishima

In Japan, there was a writer named Yukio Mishima (1925–1970). He graduated from the University of Tokyo Faculty of Law—the same faculty I graduated from.

When I was a student there, one of the law professors said something like, "Mr. Hiraoka's papers were absolutely magnificent," using Mishima's real last name Hiraoka. It was easy for the professor to make such a remark because

Mishima's reputation as a writer was already established and Mishima was well-known at that time. But it is a little doubtful whether he truly felt that way when he first read Mishima's papers. Maybe the professor just wanted to boast about having taught Mishima.

Although the professor said that Mishima's papers were always excellent, as far as I can tell from reading Mishima's novels, his works do not give the slightest impression that the author was a graduate of the Faculty of Law—there is no trace of it at all. His writing did not seem any different from the writing of someone else who has never studied law.

If you have studied law, you usually cannot write very interesting novels, except for crime fiction. You could write stories about arresting criminals, putting them on trial, and throwing them in prison but not much else. Your writing would become too specialized and therefore be uninteresting. But I did not get that kind of impression from Yukio Mishima's novels at all, so it is almost certain he was not serious about studying law. Even so, the law professor said in retrospect that Mishima wrote fine papers.

I do not know what professors say about me at the University of Tokyo now. They may be saying something like, "I couldn't read the handwriting of Ryuho Okawa's papers at all" [*laughs*].

To make your talents bloom

I have digressed a little, but my point here is that your talents will not bloom easily unless you encounter a field that suits you.

I, myself, studied law and the related fields during my university days, but I was more attracted to philosophical matters and did not find the field of law to be a perfect match for me. In fact, in carrying out my current work, I was greatly influenced by the books I read as my hobby outside of my schoolwork when I was a student and the books I read after work as an adult.

4

Encountering Books
You Can Read Repeatedly

The influence of the books I read in my 20s

Looking back, I had a very good memory in my 20s. Even decades later, I still clearly remember the contents of the books I read in my school days or during the first five years after I graduated from university. I continued to read many books after that, but I tend to forget the contents much faster and instead remember the things from my older memories better.

When I was younger, I would buy books with the little money I had at the time, and the contents of those books have lingered in my memory longer and have had a great influence on my views on life and ways of thinking. When I reread the books I had read decades ago, I can see that I have been immensely influenced by them. In those days, I would read the books that were not directly related to my school study or career; I would read them not for the sake of appearances but out of pure interest and curiosity, so much of the content has remained with me.

I also studied religion while I was working at a company. Because the contents of the books were completely unrelated to the work I was doing at the company, I read the books as a break from work and as a hobby. But those books have helped me develop the abilities I currently use.

The advantage of paper books that e-books do not have

As a young man, I struggled to find the money, place, and time to read; in other words, I had trouble saving money to buy books, securing a place to store them, and finding the time to read them. Because I could not easily expand my reserves of these three things, I was unable to stand in an advantageous position in relation to others. I could not move out of a studio apartment of about 10 square meters (108 square feet) until I was almost 30 years old, so I struggled a lot.

Nowadays, there are iPads and other electronic appliances that allow people to read e-books easily, so perhaps there is no need to store a collection of paper books. Such devices are quite beneficial for people who do not have enough space to store books, and I think it is better to have such devices than to not read books at all. However, these devices obviously have their drawbacks as well.

The greatest advantage about paper books is that the books you read and reread can still be beneficial decades later. There is great power in having books you have underlined with your own hand.

For example, it may take you three hours to read a 200-page book the first time, but if you underline the important parts, you just need to read the underlined parts the second time. Then you can grasp the main points of the book in about one-tenth of the time it took you the first time. As you reread the book a second or third time, you can add your own marks— such as bowed lines in the margins, red circles, double circles, or yellow, blue, or red markers—on the parts that are particularly important among the parts that you underlined the first time. You can also use colored sticky notes. It is similar to the way of studying from textbooks for an exam. This way, you can save even more time.

It may take a few hours—or more than 10 hours depending on the book—to read a book the first time.

But when you read the book for the second or third time, or when you want to use it for your work, you can quickly grasp the main ideas of the book in a relatively short time. This is the advantage of paper books. While I do not necessarily deny the use of e-books and other electronic appliances, please note that paper books have such benefits.

When reading contributes to work

Most of the books that I found to be beneficial were the ones I read not just once but over and over again. You cannot effectively use the ideas you gain from books in your work unless you read them repeatedly. In most cases, you need to read the books at least three times to assimilate the ideas.

There are many books I have read repeatedly; there are many I have read over 10 times. If I read them many times, I can memorize most of the important points. Once I have them memorized, I can freely use the information at any time, so it is very beneficial.

When I give a lecture, I do not use any notes. It is my policy to use only what is in my mind. I believe any information that does not linger in my memory is either not for me or unnecessary for me. The truly important information will surely stick in my mind, so I tell myself I do not need to remember the content that does not remain no matter how many times I read it. So when I refer to the content of a book in my lecture, I always speak from what I remember.

There is another advantage to reading a book repeatedly and closely. Sometimes the way you understand a book can change over time as you become more mature. In most cases, the authors of the books you read in youth are decades older than you. So when you go back and reread the books after having grown up and gained more knowledge, you will be able to pick up on the details you could not understand before. As you read more books, you will also be able to notice how some authors just skillfully paraphrase the ideas by another author. Being able to understand the content in more detail is also one of the true pleasures of reading books.

The reading style to create a highly knowledgeable and cultured person

There was a man who stated something along the lines of, "You can be a truly knowledgeable and cultured person if you read 500 favorite books repeatedly in your lifetime, so this should be one of your goals of life." This means reading 500 books over and over again will make you a very educated person.

It is certainly difficult to find 500 books that you can read repeatedly. Normally, people are busy reading new books, so they cannot read so many books repeatedly. But if you have 500 books that you can read repeatedly over the years, you can call yourself a first-rate cultured person and avid reader. But paradoxically you need to read many books to find the books you can read repeatedly.

Reading English books is also beneficial when English is your second language. If you underline the key points when reading an English book for the first time, then you can easily skim those parts later and get a general idea of the book in one-tenth or even less of the time it took you to read it the first time. In this way, owning books is very important; it allows you to grasp the general ideas of the books easily.

5
How to Find Books to Read

How to find books to read (1)
—Look for books by authors you like

Practically speaking, we have limited time to read books. In the survey I mentioned in the beginning of this chapter, there were questions from young people on how to find the books they should read. It is actually difficult to find the books you should read, but there are a few ways to do this.

One way is to read books written by your favorite authors. As you read many books, you will most likely find authors you like, so try to read different books by these authors. If you seek for books written by specific authors, you will gradually come to acquire their thoughts and ideas as your own. This style of reading is very effective in developing your ability.

Next, try to read the books that attract your interest among the books cited or listed as references in those authors' books. The authors were probably inspired by those books philosophically, so it is a good idea to read them, too.

How to find books to read (2)
—"Vine-pulling" reading method

Another method is the "vine-pulling" reading method, which was proposed by the late Hitoshi Takeuchi (1920–2004), a geophysicist and professor emeritus of the Faculty of Science at the University of Tokyo. He explored various other fields outside of physics. In a book, he introduces the "vine-pulling" reading method—a way to successively read books as if pulling a potato vine.

When you read a book, you usually come across a new topic that piques your interest. So you go on to read books about topics you are newly interested in. If you come across another topic that interests you, you move on to read books on that topic. In this way, you read books on your interest, one after another, as if pulling a potato vine.

This is also an effective way of finding books to read. This method is basically suitable for random reading, but it is especially effective when you want to expand your network of information. In this style of reading, you do not need to read books closely; it is enough just to read through them once.

How to find books to read (3)
—Focus on the table of contents and
the first chapter

There is yet another way to read books, suggested by the writer Hisashi Inoue (1934–2010). He has already passed away, but apparently he had a private collection of about 130,000 books when he was alive. This is not an amount one can read effortlessly; he must have been living with a "mountain of books."

As one way of reading books, he suggested reading the table of contents and the first chapter very carefully. Read the table of contents and the first chapter carefully and at a normal pace, so you can understand the content properly. Then, appraise the book to a certain extent. Once you have a general idea of what the author is trying to say, read at a faster pace starting from the second chapter and finish the rest of the book quickly. This was how he read books.

It is certainly true that carefully reading the table of contents and the first chapter will allow you to gain a sense of the value of the book. If, at that point, you find the book not worth reading, you can of course stop reading there. I was amazed by this method when I first learned about it. Even if you normally read books very quickly, try to read the first chapter a little more carefully; then, you will probably be able to better understand the value of the book.

The art of speed reading acquired through training

As for myself, I can read a Japanese paperback in less than 10 minutes, so even if I am told to read the first chapter slowly, I cannot. I read an entire book in about 10 minutes while underlining the important points, so it is clear I read at a very fast pace. This is not due to some supernatural power; it is the product of my training. As a result of my training, I became able to read a vast portion of the text at a glance.

When I was a college student, I could only read one row at a time, but eventually I could read two rows at a time, and then three. After that, I could read an entire page in a flash, and now, I can read both left and right pages at the same time. In other words, I look at the right page with my right eye and the left page with my left eye and read both pages at the same time. I do this as I quickly underline important points on both sides. I am able to read both left and right pages as one screen, as if I am watching a movie. When I do this, the letters of the important parts appear as if they are floating up.

Ryotaro Shiba described the text "standing up"

The Japanese writer Ryotaro Shiba (1923–1996), who died in 1996, made a similar comment. He read a great deal of material to write many historical novels. According to what he said, when he went into his library and opened a book, the text would stand up from the page. He said the text would stand up as if to say, "Read me," which sounds like a 3D film. It is a witty description. I wish I could say the same. Even I have not felt the text standing up, so I thought it was a witty way to put it.

I am not really sure if the text truly appeared to him in that way or if it was just a literary expression of how he felt, but for him, only the parts that were necessary for his work would rise up perfectly on their own accord and stand out in the material. That is really wonderful. Much like Ryotaro Shiba, some people can see the important points standing out while they flip through the pages.

In a sense, this is the result of vocational training. Professionals in all fields gain similar abilities. For example, a dentist would be able to immediately identify which tooth is bad, and a fishmonger would be able to understand the condition of the fish at a glance. A doctor would know right away about the disease he or she specializes in. A brief look at the shadow on an X-ray would be enough for a medical specialist to identify the suspicious areas, whereas an ordinary person would not understand anything at all. So there must be skills people are particularly good at in each profession.

6

Aim to Read Two Thousand Books a Year

Increase the number of pages you can read per hour

Let me introduce how I read books. In fact, I do not spend a lot of time reading books. I keep a record of the dates and the titles of the books I read in my notebook, and I also keep a tally in my calendar, which is in the same notebook. I have kept doing this for years. I do not read more than 200 books a month—I think I read around 170 books on average. Based on this, you can estimate that I read about 2,000 books a year (as of May 2018). But I do not spend much time reading. I do not read books all day long; I simply read very fast. This is the result of years of training.

It has already been several decades since I started such training. When I was a freshman in university, my average reading speed was 60 pages per hour, which is not particularly fast or slow. I am sure you would be able to read 60 pages in an hour if you tried. But my reading speed gradually increased from about 60 pages in the beginning to 70, 80, 100, and then to 120 pages per hour. Currently, I am able to read as much as I want within a specific time frame I set for myself. As a result of this training, I can now read about 2,000 books a year.

My morning routine

In Japan, over 100 new books are published every day. The realm of my specialties has been expanding, so most of the books I now read are the ones I find within my network of information.

I also read nine newspapers every morning: six Japanese newspapers—*The Asahi Shimbun, The Yomiuri Shimbun, The Sankei Shimbun, Nihon Keizai Shimbun* (Nikkei), *The Mainichi Shimbun,* and *The Tokyo Shimbun*—and *The International New York Times, Financial Times,* and *Wall Street Journal.* (Note: As of May 2018, three German newspapers were added to this list.) I also read both weekly and monthly magazines, along with some English magazines.

When I read newspapers either in Japanese or English, I listen to CNN at the same time. In other words, I listen to CNN using my ears while reading the newspapers with my eyes. I need to increase my efficiency to this extent to get through all the news.

If you read about six newspapers, you rarely miss any information about what is happening in Japan and the world right now, and you can generally make an accurate prediction from the information you read. Skimming through six papers will allow you to get a general idea of what is going on. In addition, if you read English newspapers or watch CNN or BBC, you will also be able to cover foreign news that is missing from the Japanese newspapers and understand almost everything that is happening in the world. When it comes to the news of foreign countries in particular, it is often easier to understand it through visual images than printed information, so television is also very useful.

Other than the news, I check the TV section of the newspaper for some good special programs on national or private TV stations. I check for programs about the topics I need to study, such as the economy or international affairs, and have my secretaries record them for me.

Check for newly published books

The Japanese newspapers have advertisements of newly published books in the bottom section, so I usually mark the books I want to read with a red pencil. Then, my secretaries buy them for me. However, the books I have to read start to accumulate and form a "mountain of books," so this is a little difficult to deal with at times.

In the past, I bought well over 10,000 books in one year at the most. But I realized it was too much, so now I have reduced the number of books I buy to a few thousand a year. Even so, it is still a lot of books.

Books disappear from bookstores shortly after they first come out; they often disappear within a month. So if you find books on interesting topics or ones you may need in the future, you need to get them when they are released. Once the books are gone from the bookstores, you need to search for them in used bookstores. That is why I constantly check for newly published books.

My aspiration to own a private library

I am now able to lead this lifestyle because, fortunately enough, I aspired to live a life with books when I was young. I used to have a leftist mentality until high school, but I realized I needed money to buy books and the space to store the books. Benjamin Franklin (1706–1790) said, "Time is money," but we also need money to save time. So I aspired to live a life with books when I was a university student.

In those days, I was living in a 10-square-meter studio apartment, so I struggled with finding enough space to put the many books I had. Especially when I first started living on my own, I had no refrigerator, no air conditioner, no fan, and almost no electrical appliances. Even so, there still was not enough space to store my books, so I would lay them on the floor and sleep on them.

When I was working in a trading company, I lived in a dormitory in Nagoya City and in Chiba Prefecture. My room back then was always like a "fortress of books"; when I was in my room, I could only sit at my desk or lie on the bed. In this way, I struggled to secure space and was keenly aware that I needed to earn a good amount of money and succeed in business to make enough space for my books.

The aspiration I had as a young man of around 20 years of age has been fulfilled, and I now own my private library rather than a study. Magnificently enough, the library is equipped with open bookshelves that display the spines of the books, just like a school or public library.

Normal avid readers cannot afford such luxury, so many of them pile their books on the floor. When the books are piled up, it is sometimes difficult to get hold of the book they want because removing the book at the bottom of the pile would cause all the books to topple over like a game of Jenga. So they often end up buying the same book again.

In contrast, I now have a space where I can arrange the books on an open shelving system; I have even taken measures against earthquakes so that the bookshelves do not collapse. In this way, every single book is "available" for use. There is a big difference between books being "available" and "unavailable"; even if a person has 100,000 books, if he or she can only access 10,000 books, then the remaining 90,000 books are useless.

Therefore, it was greatly significant for me to realize at a young age that money is necessary to secure space for books. I have thus managed to achieve my goal in this respect.

7

How to Increase Intellectual Productivity to Improve Your Work

What kinds of books you should read when you are young?

Judging from the number of books I have in my library, I know I will not run out of ideas for writing books even when I am 80 years old. Because I constantly take an interest in new topics and expand my area of knowledge, I know I can continue my intellectual work for as long as I want.

In recent years, Happy Science has been expanding its "battlefront" and carrying out various projects. This has become possible only because we first narrowed down the field of activity and completed the foundation as if building up blocks one by one, which I mentioned in the second section of this chapter. Without doing so, it is impossible.

Sometimes you have to give up on certain things and master each field one at a time. If you just aim to collect a lot of books to write something, you could end up being like a magazine reporter. Magazine reporters may read many books, but as they focus on reading miscellaneous books, they become unable to write anything worth reading or produce good output.

To be able to write good pieces, you need to read good books. What is more, you need to read them while you are still young and unknown. Books themselves are inexpensive compared to other things. In youth, it is extremely important to carefully read books reputed to be classics, which are often affordable. Such efforts will surely bear fruits later on in life.

"Intellectual digestion" will improve your work performance

When we conducted a survey in 2010 on some of the students among Happy Science believers, it statistically showed that the average number of books they had read so far was 243. The person who read the most had read 2,000 books. This is the number of books I read in a year. At that time, I had already written more than 700 books (over 2,850 books as of August 2021), which means that an average student had not read as many books as I had written.

It goes without saying that it takes more time to write a book than to read it. But these are also the results of accumulated effort; like a ripple effect, the more you read or write, the easier it will be for you to do those things. It feels taxing in the beginning, but as you become more proficient and gain more knowledge, you will be able to read or write more rapidly. Your work ability will also improve along the way. Once you know how to work, you will be able to quickly grasp things intellectually and master things in a short period of time.

In relation to the title of this chapter, one way to power up your intellectual strength is to train your brain to absorb and digest knowledge to a greater extent. When taking in an increasing amount of knowledge, people normally become overwhelmed and fail to digest all the information. So you need to train your brain to develop a greater ability to digest knowledge.

Another way to power up your intellectual strength is to output the knowledge you have digested. It is important to output what you digested in a form of "a product," whether through a project, work, or a lecture, thereby producing more value.

The secret of never running out of ideas in projects and other work

When outputting what you have studied, it is essential to not hold back. When you have learned valuable knowledge, you may want to keep it to yourself, but this attitude is not good. When you think you have learned something important, please output it by talking to someone about it or writing about it. You may worry you might lose your best ideas by outputting them, but without making a "vacuum state" in your mind, you will not be able to absorb anything new. So always try to output the best of what you have. Then you will have an empty space for new ideas to come in.

I, myself, do not hold back. I always output what I believe is most important from what I have learned, felt, thought, and understood as the Truth. I never worry about running out of seeds of ideas in the future.

Always output what you think is the best. Then, you will be able to create new and better ideas. If you treasure an idea and keep it to yourself without outputting it, you will become unable to absorb any new ideas. So "intellectual discharge" is essential. Ingesting and egesting always work together; you need to output knowledge to take in new knowledge.

As you increase your "intellectual productivity" in this way, you will develop a higher ability to absorb knowledge. If you want to learn something new, you first need to output knowledge. It is important to output what you have learned in one way or another, whether it is through speaking, writing, or using it in your work.

8
Continue to Power Up
Your Intellectual Strength

A surprising cause of decline
in intellectual ability

In addition, please know that it takes physical strength to keep studying. People can hardly understand this while they are students, but studying actually requires physical strength.

Our physical strength declines as we get older and enter the workforce. However, many people do not realize their intellectual ability also declines at the same time. For this reason, by taking up exercise again after our 30s, we can sometimes regain our brainpower and suddenly develop the ability to absorb more knowledge.

In Japan, college students usually have physical education classes as part of their liberal arts requirement during their first and second year, so they exercise to some extent. But they no longer have such classes in their third and fourth year. If they focus on studying without doing any exercise, they will find that they have difficulty absorbing the material no matter how hard they study. Some people spend a lot of time studying but cannot absorb what they study. In many cases, this is due to the lack of exercise.

Develop the habits to maintain your ability to absorb knowledge

By exercising, you will have less time to study when looking at it from a short-term perspective, but your ability to absorb knowledge will increase.

In my case, for example, I intentionally do some kind of exercise, such as walking or swimming, when my brain gets tired. I feel like I am losing one or two hours when I am exercising, but in reality, my ability to absorb knowledge increases tremendously after that. When I simply cannot feel motivated, I go see a movie. I have probably seen more movies than most young people today. I have probably seen almost all the movies that played in the theaters in Japan and were a big hit.

Even with the amount of work and studying I do, I still have enough time to watch movies; I have seen almost all popular and well-received movies. These movies have unknowingly served to create the foundation for me to make various films at Happy Science. By watching a movie, I have less time to study, but this change of pace allows me to read a lot of text after that.

The additional benefit of watching movies

I usually watch movies for a change of pace, but because I often watch Western movies, I am able to learn English at the same time. Although I do not necessarily make a conscious effort, I have come to understand English better as I watch more movies.

I once read an article in a weekly magazine about a person who scored a perfect score of 990 on the TOEIC English test.[2] Surprisingly, he said he cannot understand all the conversations in Western movies and cannot understand everything in the English newspapers. I remember being very surprised to read that even someone with a perfect TOEIC test score does not have very high English proficiency in reality.

I, myself, can catch almost all the English conversations in Western movies. I can understand almost everything that is said in the movie maybe because I watch so many Western movies. I do not have any difficulty reading English newspapers, either. So the article in the weekly magazine surprised me. While I watch a lot of movies for fun, my English ability has also improved without me realizing it.

It is generally said that even people who have passed Grade 1 of the Eiken test[3] can only catch about 50–60 percent of the conversations in Hollywood movies, so the article I read must have been true. In contrast, I can catch 95–100 percent of the conversations—maybe 98–99 percent on average—which means my English ability has improved considerably. I just enjoy watching the movies, but it has helped me develop my English proficiency to quite an extent.

So please know that your overall academic ability can develop in many ways by combining various activities. You can increase the "density" of your life in this way.

Learn and practice the way to grow rich

I talked about various topics in this chapter. I hope you will read it while underlining the key points. With so many topics, you may have felt that some of the ideas contradict each other and are not clear, but I described many truly important points.

After all, I talked about how you can become a millionaire in the years to come. You may not have fully grasped it yet, but you can truly grow rich by practicing what I have described here. I taught the ways to become a successful person at work and in other aspects of life as well. I believe you have yet to master them all. Even practicing a fragment of what I have described will certainly put you on the way to success.

TRANSLATOR'S NOTE

1 The 80/20 rule, otherwise known as the "Pareto principle," states that the key 20 percent determines the 80 percent of the total achievement. Refer to *The Heart of Work: 10 Keys to Living Your Calling* (New York: IRH Press, 2016).

2 The Test of English for International Communication (TOEIC) is an international standardized test of English language proficiency for non-native speakers.

3 The Eiken Test in Practical English Proficiency is an English language test conducted by a Japanese public-interest incorporated foundation, the Eiken Foundation of Japan, and backed by the Japanese Ministry of Education, Culture, Sports, Science, and Technology.

Human Growth

When you are young,
It is all the more important to study diligently.
Learn a great amount of knowledge
Quickly and accurately,
And train your brain.
First, aim to be intelligent, talented, and eloquent.

However,
Do not be satisfied at that level.
An eloquent, talented person tends to be narrow-minded.
This is not enough to be a leader.
Aim to be a big-hearted and cheerful person
Who does not fret over small details.
Develop a broad-minded and dynamic character.
Train yourself to have strong nerves.
This is the second goal.

And as the third goal,
Cultivate a composed, unwavering, and calm attitude,
And develop a dignified and reliable character.
Aim to be a magnanimous person,
A person with an unshakable mind.

Know that when evaluating people,
Those with an unshakable mind come first,
Those with a broad and dynamic mind come second,
And those with intelligence, talent,
And eloquence come third.

Refer to *Shen Yin Yu*, by Kun Lu

CHAPTER THREE

The Power of Perseverance

Mindset and Strategies to Keep Succeeding

Lecture given on August 24, 2017,
at the Special Lecture Hall of Happy Science, Japan

1

"Success in Youth" and "Success in Life"

Achieving success in youth is like a short-distance race

This chapter is on the power of perseverance. Although I have written a book titled *The Laws of Perseverance* (Tokyo: HS Press, 2014), I have never given a lecture on the power of perseverance itself. It is an easy and simple theme, but I believe I need to talk about the power of perseverance as a teaching of the mind. This topic bears important points on how to succeed not only in one's youth but also after a certain age.

There is a time limit to be successful in youth. You have to think about how to achieve a set goal or overcome challenges within a certain time limit. So it is a race against time. If you can overcome those challenges and achieve your goal faster than others, you will be admired and praised as brilliant, highly talented, or a genius. This can determine the course of your life thereafter.

Take, for example, someone who aims to be a professional baseball player. He will not attract the attention of scouts and get a chance to try out for professional baseball unless he achieves remarkable results in national tournaments while in high school. Of course, there may be cases in which excellent players on unknown local teams are individually scouted. But in most cases, it is rare for someone to become a professional baseball player with a sign-on bonus of hundreds of thousands or millions of dollars if they did not achieve outstanding results on the big stage from early on.

The same can be said of those in the entertainment business. Unless you attract people's attention in your teens or early 20s, it is difficult to become a professional singer, actor, or any other kind of entertainer. There are certainly people who start their careers after their early 20s, but these are exceptions. In reality, it is hard to remain in show business unless you aim for it from a relatively young age.

The same is true for a professional *shogi* (Japanese chess) player as well. You have to stand out by rapidly climbing the ranks from a relatively young age. It will be difficult to make a living as a professional shogi player unless one can swiftly reach at least the fourth *dan* (level).

Achieving success in youth is like a short-distance race; it is as if you are being tested to see whether you can break 10 seconds in a 100-meter race. The difference of 0.1 seconds in one's youth can actually lead to the difference of a hundred thousand or a million dollars in his or her future income.

Is the "race of life" a short-distance or long-distance race?

Now, let us view life on a longer time span of several decades.

To run a 100-meter dash, even a slow runner would be able to complete the race in no more than 20 seconds. I have not run a 100-meter dash for a long time, so I am not sure how fast I can run now. But I am sure it would not take longer than 20 seconds, even if I run at my own pace. A world-class sprinter would only take about 10 seconds to reach the goal, whereas a slow, middle-aged man would take about 20 seconds. So the difference between the two would be no more than 10 seconds.

Such time difference is inevitable in a race that is measured at a certain point, but the "race of life" is a little different from normal races. There may be a big difference in mental strength between people, but the difference in physical strength—the difference of running a 100-meter dash in 10 or 20 seconds—does not matter so much if the purpose of exercising is to maintain one's physical health. It simply depends on how you control the pace.

Those who can run a 100-meter dash in 10 seconds are very athletic and must have trained their bodies well. But it does not necessarily mean that athletes with well-trained bodies can perform well throughout their lives; they could damage or hurt a part of their body and unexpectedly lead a miserable life later on. This may be because they had pushed themselves too much.

Some people may think they are not smart or successful unless they can achieve their goals in a short time. But this is not necessarily true if you view life as a long-distance race. Judging your abilities within a short time frame is not necessarily the royal road to understanding life; it is a mere introduction to the study of life.

What happens to those who achieved too big a success in their youth?

In general, those who display smartness, talents, or a high IQ at an early age tend to achieve success easily. This is certainly true. In the U.S., for example, prodigies can enter university in their early teens and hold a teaching position by the age of 20 or so, unlike in Japan. Such people must have been smart when they were young. However, some who have become professors at the age of 20 can end up staying in the same position for 40 or 50 years without making any further advancement in their careers. Although talented people often walk on the path to success from a young age, they cannot easily keep succeeding for 40 or 50 years after that.

If you have goals and work hard to achieve them, like a horse running after a dangling carrot, you do not need to rush to become a professor in your early 20s. It is not too late to become a professor at the age of 40 or 50. People who have spent a longer time to become a professor have made more efforts during that time, so they could have more achievements in the end.

Many of the professors I had during my university days were the type of people who entered the path to success at a relatively young age. They were brilliant in their youth, wrote a thesis equivalent to a doctoral dissertation about three years after graduating from university, and elaborated on the content of the thesis to publish their first academic books around the age of 30. However, they would stop publishing books after that. For some professors, it was the only book they published, whereas others published a total of two books, including the book they wrote when they became a professor. In either case, they only published a few books. They must have worked hard to write these highly specialized and detailed books, but they were probably not persistent enough to keep producing books for a long time.

The "formula of success" is not limited only to youth

There is a saying, "You never forget your own trade," but there are many people who expect to get ahead in life only using their past achievements as a "free pass." To use the previous example of the 100-meter dash, some people who crossed the finish line faster than others and won the 10-second race may be hopeful that the trophy or the gold medal they got will ensure their livelihood for the rest of their lives or serve as a useful qualification. I think many people who worked much harder than others in their youth think in this way.

Although things do not necessarily go as they wish in reality, they try to cross the finish line early and get on the fast track in hopes of automatically rising to success, as if riding on an escalator. There have been many such people since the old days. But if an age when many people think in this way continues for a long time, fewer outstanding people will emerge.

On the other hand, heroes often appear in times when a country is in a state of disorder, has problems in politics, in the economy, or in other fields, or confronts a huge emerging evil. The Warring States period is one example of this.

So, the "formula of success" is not only limited to youth. Even if you did not achieve good results in your youth, do not label or limit yourself too much.

2

True Intelligence as a Human

A difficult editorial written by a famous scholar

I once read an editorial written by a famous scholar in the evening paper of a major newspaper. I read it a few times because it was about politics, foreign diplomacy, and international issues—topics I often talk about in my lectures. But I could not understand what he was trying to say.

Perhaps I read too fast to catch the meaning, so to make an objective judgment, I asked Shio Okawa, Aide to Master, to read the editorial thoroughly to see if she could understand it. After reading it carefully about three times, she said she could not understand what it was trying to say, either. It was written by a famous scholar, but we still could not comprehend it regardless of whether we read it quickly or slowly.

The scholar had interspersed the knowledge he has throughout his writing to answer to potential criticisms from both sides, but there was no conclusion to his editorial. He presented various possible arguments on different matters but did not make any conclusions. He used difficult words and information here and there to look insightful and dignified, but his way of writing was too difficult to understand from just one reading. Perhaps he believes writing incomprehensible essays helps him maintain his authority or status.

I have read this type of difficult papers, books, and textbooks since I was young, but I have always had an odd feeling about them. On the day I read the editorial, I spent hours trying to figure out what he was driving at as I went to sleep at night. This experience especially made me wonder what it means to be "intelligent" when one is around 20 years old. I get the feeling that the criteria for judging intelligence out in society are somewhat different from the ones used in school.

Intelligence at school and intelligence out in society

As you study at school and learn more difficult and abstract material, learn more difficult words, and become capable of writing difficult essays that others cannot understand from reading once, you may feel you have become rather intelligent. But where can you use this "intelligence" out in society? You may be able to use it at the courthouse or government offices. Perhaps you can use it in research-related jobs as well. However, I doubt it is of much use in other fields.

There was a Japanese TV drama called *My Loser Husband*, in which the main character works at an event planning company. What would happen if a so-called intelligent person were to be assigned work involving public relations or the task of planning a town revitalization project, for example? In most cases, the person would end up being incompetent.

In general, your mission at work is to make an impact on as many people as possible in an easy-to-understand way so that they will participate in, get involved in, or use your services. So the intelligence required out in society is not about showing off; it is not about writing or saying difficult things others cannot understand or about displaying detailed knowledge others have never heard of. Rather, it is about the ability to choose what you think is best for others from the ample knowledge you have and present it in an organized way. I think these kinds of skills are not taught enough at school.

The simple truths taught in classics

People today may find it difficult to read classic books, but back in the day, those books were not necessarily considered difficult. In *The Analects*, for example, Confucius writes, "Is it not delightful to have friends come from afar?" Here, he is simply describing the joy you would naturally feel when a friend visits you from afar, especially when the transportation system was still poor. He also writes, "Isn't it a pleasure to study and practice what you have learned?" This is also an obvious statement describing the joys of reviewing what you have learned in the past. In this way, if you rephrase what is written in classic books in plain words, you will find that they are often stating very simple ideas.

People may also regard philosophy to be difficult, but this is not so hard, either. Socrates, for example, did not have any writings of his own, so the dialogues written by his student Plato have become the main source of his teachings. Many people read it in translated form and may find some expressions of the translation outdated and complicated. But because everything is written in dialogue, the content itself is not so difficult to understand.

The same can be said of Buddhist sutras. The special chanting by the Buddhist priests is often regarded as holy, but many of the original Buddhist scriptures are written in the form of dialogues between Buddha and his disciples. So I do not think they were considered to be very difficult back in the day.

So, depending on the time and place, you may find some writings difficult to understand. But I believe what have remained as universal teachings to date were originally fairly easy ideas stated using clear and precise words.

What I bear in mind when I give lectures

I, too, sometimes feel tempted and think it might be "safer" for me to say something difficult so people would not easily understand what I am saying. I feel this way especially when I try to speak about a new subject, but I now understand that my work would not be meaningful unless I speak in plain, refined words.

When I give lectures, I do not speak boastfully as if to show off my knowledge. Some people in the audience have studied my teachings for a long time, while others are listening to my lecture for the first time, so I tell myself I must satisfy both groups of people. This is a difficult challenge for me.

Although I do not want to use difficult words, there are times when I need to use specialized terms. I just mentioned that writings of scholars are often difficult to understand, but if an ordinary person attends and listens to the presentations at an academic conference or workshop targeting doctors who are researching a specific organ, for example, the person would not understand anything that is being said. This cannot be helped. There are times when you have to study specialized knowledge to understand the content that is not intended for the general public. The same can be said of other academic fields as well.

3

Three Occasions
When Your Perseverance Is Tested

*Occasionally simplify things and
remind yourself of your starting point*

My point here is this: No matter what field people are in, they become well-versed and very particular about their specializations as they make efforts and accumulate knowledge, but they have to occasionally simplify things and remind themselves of their starting point. You need to ask yourself, "Why am I studying or doing this work in the first place? What aspiration did I have when I first started?" and look back at your initial motive.

In the Diet session in Japan, for example, some government officials dodge questions skillfully so they can evade making commitments or taking responsibility and remain in office. In a way, you could call this a type of debate or consider it to be "productive," given that it guarantees them lifetime earnings. An honest answer can easily drive them out of office, so some bureaucrats probably take part in the discussions in the Diet as a kind of "intellectual game." The media, bureaucrats, and politicians use such techniques in conversation to evade responsibility, and this is probably one of the reasons why it takes so much time to make decisions and why there is much delay and little progress in Japanese politics.

The "perseverance" of the former Prime Minister Eisaku Sato

Former Japanese Prime Minister Eisaku Sato, great-uncle to former Prime Minister Abe, conducted politics in a similar way. Although young people may not know him, I have seen him in his prime.

Eisaku Sato served as prime minister for seven years and eight months, and his term in office is the longest in post-war Japan (at the time of the lecture). He was a bureaucrat turned politician, and I remember him talking about the importance of "perseverance" as well. He served as prime minister for a long time, as if to demonstrate that persevering while evading or postponing making decisions as much as possible is the key to remaining in office for a long time.

You could call this "bureaucratic-style politics." Because he avoided making mistakes by postponing making decisions, there were no incidents that forced him to leave office or instigated people's anger calling for his resignation. I had an impression that his term in office just dragged on without much progress.

A prime minister who explicitly expresses his views and confronts his opponents can become popular, but this type of leader often ends up resigning after a short time. Former Prime Minister Kakuei Tanaka was quick-witted and pushed things forward like a bulldozer, but he resigned after serving for only about two years.

On the contrary, those who do not clearly express their opinions can unexpectedly remain in office for a long time. It is difficult to tell whether this is because they are simply incompetent or whether it is the result of their perseverance. But at the very least, they must have strong mental strength to be able to do so.

Continued success requires perseverance rather than talent

Some people continue to do their job at a constantly high level for a long period of time or constantly produce good results. It must have taken a lot of time for them to acquire the ability to do so, but recently I keenly feel this is also a kind of talent. Many people want to succeed quickly, but if they easily get bored, they will try something new one after another as soon as they achieve a certain level of success in one field and will often end up not attaining great success. In this sense, gifted people do not necessarily achieve great success. This is because they lack perseverance.

Perseverance is a great power, but this is something people do not learn easily when they are young. Children may endure being scolded by their parents or schoolteachers, or they may endure being trained by a club supervisor or a coach. In most cases, what people persevere during youth is the mental fatigue of studying or the aching muscle from training.

Take, for example, the training of a baseball team. A high school baseball team in Saitama Prefecture in Japan won the championship at the summer national tournament in 2017. Originally, they were not a very strong team. They were weak on offense, so they set a goal of acquiring "destructive power" and introduced new drills in their winter training. Apparently, the new drills involved hitting tires with a big hammer and running in traditional Japanese rubber-soled cloth footwear to develop greater sensitivity in the soles of their feet. These exercises seem primitive, but they had a positive effect on the baseball players.

Happy Science Academy in Nasu also has a baseball team. They were always losing by the mercy rule, so they asked me what they should do to win. I recommended that they go on more runs and strengthen their muscles more during the winter. Then, in the following year, they started to win. Happy Science Academy is not a big school, and half of the student body consists of female students, so it must be quite a challenge for them to make their way to the national tournament. But after I gave them some advice, the team rapidly became stronger and came close to winning a championship in the local tournament.

I am an amateur in terms of baseball, but after I advised them to run more and do more strength training in the winter to gain sharper batting skills and improve their batting average, they truly became stronger. While it is important to devise new ways to improve your ability and consider what to do, you need to persevere through the tough times and keep training yourself.

The difficulty of making continuous efforts in ordinary life

As I mentioned earlier, some genius-type people become associate professors or professors soon after graduating from university, but they eventually reach a plateau in their career and stop producing positive results for decades. As a result, the book they wrote in their 20s can often end up being the only major work they accomplish in their career.

It is a little sad if genius-type people quickly disappear from the spotlight like a short-lived sparkler. So you need to think about how to make your entire life more fruitful and make efforts to achieve it.

In the long run, intelligence in youth is not such a big deal. One's intelligence could be roughly classified into the high, middle, or low level, but some students get good marks in exams because they happened to study a particular section or because they crammed before the exam. They cannot continue to succeed for the rest of their lives with the same know-how they used to succeed in school.

Basically, it is important to achieve success through the royal road of studying or working. Along the way, there will be times when you lead an ordinary life, when you have to go against headwind, or when you are on the crest of a wave. Knowing how to cope with each occasion is an extremely difficult challenge.

In fact, persevering in difficult times can sometimes be easier. For example, when a family is burdened with debt, it is often said that siblings and other family members are easily united. The more members there are to shoulder the burden, the lighter the load for each person will be, so everyone strives to work together. On the contrary, when one of them gets a big sum of money through something like the lottery, it is said that the family relationship goes sour. In this case, the fewer family members they have the better because there will be more money split per person.

After all, persevering in times of hardship may not be so hard because you are prepared to bear the situation to some extent. Rather, your patience can wear out when you have to lead a mundane life for 10 years.

There is an infinite number of people who work hard to be recognized in a short period of time but fade from the limelight once they achieve good results and attract people's attention. Even people who were once in the spotlight or were the talk of the town are forgotten in one or two years' time. There are countless cases like this.

The same is true in the world of new religions. In Japan, many new religious groups emerged around the 1980s. Some became famous or popular for a certain period of time, but after 30 years, most of them have disappeared or are on the verge of disappearing.

Happy Science was founded around the same time. Back in the day, some religious groups appeared to us like big corporations or well-established groups that had lasted for decades or even 100 years. But now, we have developed so much that they have come to appear small to us without our realizing it. This means we have made steady efforts not only when we were in the spotlight or were the target of criticisms but also in ordinary, day-to-day life. We have continued to think about what to work on next when we appeared to have achieved our goals from an objective perspective. These are the key points to bear in mind.

When the talent you thought to be insignificant turns into your power

Highly intelligent people can anticipate the potential outcome too quickly and end up giving things up too easily. Perhaps it is one type of intelligence to be able to see the potential failure at an early stage and stop oneself from taking on the challenge. However, when tackling an issue that is not totally impossible and when there is a slight chance of success, it is quite difficult to determine how long you should persevere to accomplish it.

Even if you think you do not have much talent, as long as you have a quality that hints at talent even a little, hold onto it and persevere. Then, before you know it, that talent will develop into something much greater. Sometimes, the skill you acquired can bring out a talent that you thought was insignificant.

In a fight or competition where there is a clear winner and loser, you should fight with your strengths as much as possible. But once you have achieved some success, you need to work on the other abilities you considered to be not as significant. Then, you will find that they, too, can become your strengths. This is worth noting.

4

Reading Techniques to Develop Character and Work Ability

How to read books to develop basic abilities

I have written many books, including the ones to be used at Happy Science University (HSU); the books cover the basic attitude for learning and many other topics. Because I have always taught the importance of reading many books, some people may simplistically jump to a conclusion and think they can be successful by collecting many books in their youth. But I must say this is not exactly true.

Young people need strategies specific to youth. For example, many students depend on the money sent by their parents, scholarship, or earnings at a part-time job to make their living, and they often do not have ample funds to spend. It takes a lot of effort for them to squeeze money out of their tight budget and buy books, but they can gain a sense of accomplishment after reading the books they obtained in this way. Each book they read will be engraved in their memory.

I continued to read many books after I started to work in society, but I remember the ones I read as a student more clearly. As a student, I did not have extra money to spend on books, so I tried very hard to make the most of the books I bought and to get my money's worth. I would say to myself, "I bought this book when I could have bought a Hamburg steak. It would be a waste if I leave it unread." Such thoughts motivated me to read. When I could not understand certain books after reading them once, I read them again and again on different occasions or until I could fully assimilate the content. These efforts largely helped me develop my basic abilities.

Reading in youth is different from reading as an adult

If you are a professional writer or have a job involving information processing, it is of course important to own many books as reference material even if you do not actually read them all. Having books on your specialty alone will be greatly helpful, so once you establish yourself in a field of work and come to earn a decent income, you need to collect as many books that are relevant to your work as possible. Some people need to have reference books at hand so they can look up information in those books as necessary.

During youth, however, you should not simply focus on owning many books. When you are young, it is more important to establish a foundation of knowledge and nourish your soul through reading. As you read different books, your "antenna" will catch certain kinds of information, which is often related to your future work. So try to find those kinds of books as much as possible.

Such books usually reflect the authors' views on life or ways of thinking, and some novels have themes or characters that you can relate to. In the case of books on historical figures, you can learn their ways of thinking or how they overcame adversities in life. So when you read books during youth, it is better to absorb the essence of the book and gain ideas that have a positive influence on your character.

Select information for reading and at work

Once you enter the workforce and come to deal with various kinds of information, you may have to process information differently than you did as a student. When the information you deal with becomes too diverse, you need to narrow it down occasionally. Focus on what needs to be learned and study it carefully while spending less time on information that is only needed for reference.

People such as magazine reporters have to read many popular books as well as newspapers. They may have to watch the news on TV and read the magazines published by their competitors. But if they only gain a large volume of miscellaneous knowledge in this way, they often end up being unproductive and just waste time, money, and space. In such cases, they need to deal with the information in a different, more appropriate way.

You may be inclined to buy weekly magazines after reading the headlines advertised in newspapers, but even if you read the actual articles, most of the time, you are unlikely to gain any information that is more meaningful than what was described in the headlines. You will most likely end up feeling that reading the headlines was enough.

The headlines are usually eye-catching, but the articles often do not contain any information more valuable than that. For example, when you read a headline that says, "Have a Broiled Eel for the Midsummer Day of the Ox (eel-eating day)," the mental image of the delicious smell of broiled eel may make you want to read the article. But it often is not something worth spending your time reading, and you end up regretting buying and reading the magazine.

There are endless cases in which your time can be wasted in this way. So when you have an increasing amount of information to deal with, it is important to make an effort to be selective.

The same is true at work. When the need arises, your work can spread out over a wide range of matters or become diversified. This is sometimes inevitable. At such times, you need to figure out the crucial points and think about what to keep in the end. At Happy Science, too, if we go into too much detail when spreading our teachings, many people might become confused about what exactly is being taught. So sometimes we must focus on the main points and make an effort to remind people of the important teachings.

5

Create a Life Strategy
Based on Perseverance

Great work cannot be achieved
without the power of perseverance

Perseverance has considerable power. If you want to accomplish the kind of work that will remain in the future, you definitely need the power of perseverance. This is because many of the works that will have a greater impact on later generations often cannot be evaluated properly in the present.

It takes courage and determination to do and accomplish work that is not valued by one's contemporaries. In addition, you need perseverance to keep doing what you are determined to do. Without perseverance, it is impossible to accomplish anything great.

At work, sometimes people who are calm and patient get ahead later in their career. This shows that they actually possess the power of perseverance. These people are often good observers. They always observe the work of others and carefully listen to what their superiors say.

At the same time, they continue to accumulate abilities by refining their skills on their own. In contrast, those who aim to achieve rapid success, which is typical of today's society, tend to rush through life as if they are aiming to attain a successful life in their 20s and die in their 40s. These types of people need to be careful not to lead such a life.

The attitude needed to prevent burnout

There are several turning points in life. You need the strength to overcome each challenge and continue working hard until you come across the next turning point.

What do you need to do during the time between these turning points? As I mentioned in section three of this chapter, it is all the more important to put your heart and soul into matters that produce positive results. At the same time, you also need to work on other abilities you see potential in. Study a subject you see potential in outside your specialty little by little, all the while devoting yourself to becoming an expert in what you are mainly pursuing.

In agriculture, for example, you can use the same farmland to grow rice twice or alternate between rice and other crops or vegetables in a single year. This is called double cropping, and some farmlands are used as both farmland and rice fields. To do this, the farmland needs to be blessed with a suitable climate, and there must be an established agricultural method as well. In the old days, when the amount of harvest dropped, farmers would let the farmland lie fallow and wait until the soil was naturally replenished by nutrients.

A similar attitude is necessary in life as well. People usually devote themselves fully and try their hardest when they have a specific goal to achieve. But just as it is said since old times, people sometimes exert themselves to the point of exhaustion and suffer from burnout syndrome. They overexert themselves and end up running out of energy. This is one of the reasons why many people who are considered to be talented disappear. These people burn out for some reason. It is like someone who runs 100 meters at top speed believing it is their last race but is then told to run another 100-meter dash; they will suddenly feel stunned and troubled.

Emma Stone, who seized her chance after auditioning numerous times

There are also the types of people such as the American actress Emma Stone, who won the Academy Award for Best Actress in a Leading Role for the movie *La La Land*. It is said that the movie partly overlaps with her experience in her younger days. In the movie, there was a scene where the protagonist works at a coffee shop while pursuing a career in acting. Apparently, Emma Stone herself experienced similarly hard times when she failed about 100 auditions. Even someone who got her big break and was called the world's highest-paid actress has had a life of obscurity for a certain period of time.

It is unbelievable that people in Hollywood did not have an eye for her talent in her earlier auditions and failed someone who later became the world's highest-paid actress. She could not have made it if she did not believe in herself, much like the protagonist in the movie who kept trying while working at a coffee shop. But in just a matter of 10 years, she won the Academy Award and became the world's highest-paid actress. No one could have anticipated that she would achieve such a big success.

There are times when your efforts do not bear fruit at all. However, various things can happen in life; a path may open after seizing an opportunity or the door to opportunity may open after encountering a particular person. But until then, you need to keep making efforts under the surface, like a waterbird paddling underwater.

Waterbirds appear beautiful and graceful above the surface of the water, but they are actually busy paddling the water with their webbed feet underneath. In the same way, humans must make efforts behind the scenes to achieve success. Even with such efforts, you cannot always achieve success, but without it, success will remain unreachable. As long as you have aspirations, and depending on the scale of your life plan, you can experience a series of successes.

Launch attacks in waves to realize a "multi-track life"

I also give teachings on business management. I have taught that there are always ups and downs in business and that businesses will eventually reach and pass a peak. So, how can you avoid having such ups and downs?

One of the ways to do this is to attack in waves. Businesses in general appear to be running numerous projects concurrently, but in most cases, they are launching them in waves. Once they release the initial "wave," they set off another wave before the first wave completely disappears, overlaying the second wave on the first. Then, they set off yet another wave to overlay on top of the preceding waves. If they repeat this process based on the theory of "attacks in waves," it will appear as if they are consistently riding the crest of the waves most of the time. Therefore, it is extremely important to constantly think about what to launch as the next wave, and the one after the next, based on the awareness that a trough will eventually follow the crest of a wave.

This is true not only in business but also in life; if you prepare for the next wave and the wave after the next, you can lead a "multi-track life." Unless such efforts are made, it would be rather difficult to remain active on the frontline for prolonged periods of time. It is also worth noting that you can train your mind and body afresh to make them more efficient no matter how old you are.

So, what factor can help develop your ability one step further? What works to boost your ability right before reaching the peak? It goes without saying that your day-to-day efforts are essential, but on top of that, you need to concentrate at the critical moment. Exerting your power of concentration and your passion is extremely important.

The power of the mind to calmly accept both successes and failures

In many cases, crisis precedes success. Ordinary people tend to be easily crushed by hardship and adversity, but you need to maintain a strong self-image of yourself withstanding adversity at a time of crisis. The power of the mind makes a big difference.

Life is not always filled with good events; rather, it has both ups and downs. You need to be aware of this. So when you are doing well and are on the rise, you have to discipline yourself so you do not become conceited and fall from grace. Your success may not be real and only temporary. Or your success may be due to the support from other people or because you luckily managed to ride the wave. You need to look at yourself from an objective and detached perspective in this way.

There are also times when you will begin to decline; you may become less popular, your business may become sluggish, or people around you may expect less from you. However, even in such a tough situation that makes ordinary people feel discouraged, it is important to grit your teeth and persevere instead of feeling too depressed.

I, myself, have always thought about how to attack in waves. I have always tried to move things forward, so my progress appears steady in the eyes of others. It is impossible to achieve success all the time, and you may fail at times. However, do not leave your failures as mere failures. Rather, think of ways to turn those failures into the seeds of your next success. I have always taken this attitude. When I find things to be going poorly because of limitations or obstacles, I always try to change my ways of thinking.

6

Perseverance for
Developing Organizations

The importance of establishing a proper style of missionary work and faith

The Happy Science Group has a political party, the Happiness Realization Party (HRP). From an objective perspective, it seems to be having a hard time gaining support. People in general may simply think it is a good idea to engage in political activities because we can spread the name of Happy Science and make it famous. However, because most of the HRP candidates are unknown, we cannot gain many votes even though we have many new candidates running for the election. Furthermore, if the candidates are not well-known within Happy Science, they cannot gain enough support even within our organization. In that sense, engaging in political activities can actually chip away at the power of our organization; sometimes we end up giving an impression that Happy Science is a small, powerless religious group. This is quite a painful situation, and we can hardly say we are successful when we only look at the activities of our political party.

What if we look at the situation from a religious point of view? People join Happy Science for many reasons; some join because they simply like religion, while others join in hopes of escaping from the suffering in life or healing their sorrows from the death of their loved ones. These kinds of people have come to us to fulfill their religious needs, so they may not immediately take interest in our political activities. Even so, as they study our teachings and take part in various activities, they may change their minds little by little. As they continue to learn about basic political knowledge over time, their enthusiasm for political activities can gradually increase.

There may be some people among our members who do not believe our teachings as completely as we would expect them to. Unlike in Islam, we at Happy Science do not force our faith on people by saying, "Your life will be taken if you break a promise with God." So there are probably many believers who pick and choose what teachings to listen to based on their own interests, regardless of the fact that these are all words of God. There are also many believers who remain dormant and inactive. In that sense, we could say that we have yet to succeed in sufficiently establishing the proper style of missionary work and faith or that our faith has yet to take root as deeply as it needs to. There may be some areas in our main work of religion that require more effort.

The importance of leading people toward faith

Japanese people, in particular, have a unique view of religion. For example, many Japanese people hold wedding ceremonies at churches in accordance with the Christian tradition, hold funeral services at temples in accordance with the Buddhist tradition, and take their children to Shinto shrines to pray for their health and well-being upon reaching the age of three, five, or seven. Even though they are not Christians, they celebrate Valentine's Day with chocolates and Christmas with cake. At Christmas, almost all Japanese appear to be Christians, but with the arrival of New Year's Day, they return to Shinto customs and visit shrines to offer their gratitude and New Year's resolutions. Because of such national characteristics, it is difficult for faith to deeply take root in people's minds like an anchor sinking into the ocean.

But this does not necessarily mean that Japanese people are non-religious; they actually have religious faith. To put it another way, Japan is like a pastry shop with different kinds of cake. You could say that Japanese people have trouble selecting a piece of cake from the many delicious pieces at the store because eating many cakes will result in excessive calorie intake and obesity. They feel like they have to pick just one among the variety of cakes, such as chocolate cake, strawberry cake, melon cake, or chestnut cake.

Some members of Happy Science may be making various choices in the same way. In that sense, we need to be more creative and give them a little more push to guide them to study important teachings and participate in major activities little by little. For example, we could recommend visiting Happy Science shoja (temples) or local branches to people by saying, "It's good to visit a shrine on the New Year's Day, but God would be too busy granting the wishes of the millions of worshippers. Why not come to the Happy Science temple instead? Your prayers are more likely to be granted there."

More honesty and cleanness are needed in politics

Looking at our political activities, some people may think we are amateurs in terms of politics because Happy Science is a religious organization. But even from an amateur's point of view, current politics is full of lies. I cannot help feeling that politicians spend too much time deceiving and lying to the people. Things will proceed more smoothly if they have a candid and straightforward discussion from the perspective of whether certain decisions were beneficial or harmful for the people or whether the central and municipal governments or local offices are dealing with problems in a fair, selfless manner. But there are many politicians who are trying hard to prevent things from proceeding smoothly.

In times like these, candidates who are honest from a religious perspective should be elected as politicians. If such candidates are not elected, it means those who criticize politicians are also in the "dirty flow" and are seeing the current situation as a matter of course. In fact, some people make a value judgment based on the idea that rivers are naturally murky. Those who have only seen the Ganges River and the Yellow River may believe that rivers are usually murky. If so, even if they are engaged in work involving rivers or fishing, they may not know that clean rivers also exist. In this sense, it is good for amateurs to get involved in politics. Their frank and straightforward opinions may sometimes persuade others to change their opinions on certain matters.

Establishing a new university is difficult in Japan—as we have seen through our difficulties of registering our university. But when I see news reports on the Kake Gakuen scandal, I sense that the process of approving a new university is also based on give and take, and those who are good at forming interest-based communities are working behind the scenes.

To establish a faculty of veterinary medicine in Ehime Prefecture, Kake Gakuen was said to have received the subsidy of up to ¥9.6 billion (about US$87 million) from the prefectural and municipal governments. The initial estimated construction cost was ¥19.2 billion (about US$175 million), so perhaps Kake Gakuen expected half of the cost to be covered by the subsidy. However, according to one source, the actual construction cost was not as expensive and was about ¥12 billion (about US$109 million), and there is an ongoing debate about whether they swindled taxpayers' money. (Note: On November 14, 2017, the Ministry of Education, Culture,

Sports, Science, and Technology announced the approval of the new faculty, the Faculty of Veterinary Medicine, at Kake Educational Institution.)

It is surprising that the school managed to get ¥9.6 billion from the prefectural and municipal governments to build its faculty of veterinary medicine. They will probably keep receiving subsidies to continue operating the school. It is unbelievable that they depend on taxpayers' money to draw up the budget to run their school. On the other hand, Happy Science has no intention of depending on subsidies to establish a university. Even so, we received a lot of restrictions and orders. While I acknowledge Kake Gakuen's ability to involve politicians, bureaucrats, and other officials to achieve their goals, their efforts seem somewhat hollow.

Self-control is all the more necessary when you achieve big success

I often watch movies because I make films as part of my work. As I watch different kinds of movies, I realized that many Japanese movies receive subsidies from the Ministry of Education, Culture, Sports, Science, and

Technology. Apparently, any Japanese movie including some aspect of the traditional arts qualifies for a subsidy. I do not know how much money filmmakers actually receive, but because it shows up in the credits so often, I presume some government officials have nothing better to do than to think about where to distribute the subsidies.

The Japanese movie *Your Name* became a huge hit between 2016 and 2017. It had a total of more than 10 million viewers in Japan alone, and the box office sales amounted to about ¥25 billion (about US$228 million). Even so, it was still subsidized. The movie probably managed to get the qualification to receive subsidies because it incorporated some aspects of Japanese traditional culture, such as *Kuchikami-sake* practiced at shrines, *kumihimo* braiding, and Japanese traditional dancing. When they were making the film, the production team apparently thought they would be lucky if the box office sales reached ¥1 billion. But the movie turned out to be a big hit. Given such success, they should have returned the subsidies, although I have no intention of making any petty remarks.

Sometimes you can achieve success with the help of external powers, but make sure not to have selfish motives in achieving success. At the same time, always check and see if your success is acceptable from the perspective of other people as well. This holds true for all kinds of work in all fields. The bigger your success is, or the more powerful and influential you become, the fairer and more selfless you should be. It is essential to strive to be egoless.

Happy Science is aiming to become a global-scale religion, so it is all the more important for us to view things with an egoless mind. We must not judge things based on worldly interests or profits. It takes perseverance to continue making an effort while controlling oneself.

7

Perseverance as a Resource of Success

In this chapter, I have talked about perseverance from various angles. Many people may believe that one's intelligence or talent determines success and happiness in life. This may certainly be true when looking at life over a short period of time. However, in the long run, even those with abundant intelligence or talent could fail; some fail in relationships, while others fail because they lack money sense. So it is important to make an effort so you can develop further no matter what happens, like a snowball getting bigger as it rolls down a hill.

Perseverance is a truly important asset for you to succeed, especially when you feel your talent or ability has yet to fully bloom or you do not have much talent. Even if you are not born with perseverance, you can acquire it through self-discipline or training. Please know this. Accumulate daily efforts to acquire this asset, and you will surely possess it. Although water will not turn to oil no matter how many times you stir it, the human mind can change if you ardently discipline yourself with a purpose.

I would also like you to know that what you find very difficult to do now will eventually become easy for you. For example, there was a professional tightrope walker who walked along a wire stretched across the Niagara Falls. Watching this, people clapped and cheered. Then a spectator said to him, "You could walk on the wire while pushing a wheelbarrow with someone in it. With your confidence, you could do it." To that he replied, "Will you ride in the wheelbarrow, then? I'm sure I can walk along the wire with you in the wheelbarrow." In the end, the person declined because it was too scary. Even if a professional tightrope walker asks someone to get in the wheelbarrow to cross the Niagara Falls, there is no guarantee they will not fall.

While it takes tremendous courage to ride in the wheelbarrow pushed by a master tightrope walker, it also takes tremendous skills to walk along the wire. As you continue doing what ordinary people usually cannot, other people will start to expect more from you. But when they are asked to do the same, they soon realize they cannot.

Different people will say many different things to you. However, focus on your efforts while being aware of your own limits. It is very important to accumulate further efforts to overcome your limits by building your intellectual and physical strengths and deepening your understanding of life. This concludes the teaching of the mind on perseverance described in simple terms.

The Way to Make the Most of Yourself

The world population is continuing to increase.
Does this mean
The value of your life
Is decreasing day by day?

No, it cannot be.
No, it should not be.
Now is the time
For many talented, brave men and women to rise.

New gods-to-be
Must be born into this world.

To put it another way,
There is an urgent need
To nurture future-oriented leaders.

Do not expect too much
From the government or the public offices.
Innovation does not arise
From sticking to past principles
And avoiding challenges.

Train your mind.
Read the stories of great figures of the past,
And hear the cries of their souls.
You, yourself, must become
A lighthouse in the dark night.

People who aspire to rise high toward heaven
Are what the world needs now.
Prove yourself as a child of God.
This is the way to make the most of yourself.

Afterword

This book, in a way, is a theory of success. But because it is based on my own abilities and experiences, it can be interpreted differently depending on the readers' abilities, talents, and experiences and on the environments they find themselves in.

Love is necessary to become a creative person. Only when you are determined to make others happy will you have the strong will to find time, to crystallize wisdom, and to make continuous, steady efforts. Money can buy you time and books, but not all people with riches become intelligent, creative people. Rather, they are more apt to become lazy.

Nevertheless, you can find the secrets to enriching your life by becoming a creative person. So I believe this book will be the power to change your future. Each and every good book I encountered has made me what I am today. In the same way, I pray this will be a life-changing book that will help my readers carve out a brighter future.

Ryuho Okawa
Master & CEO of Happy Science Group
May 16, 2018

*This book is a compilation of the lectures,
with additions, as listed below.*

- Chapter One -

How to Become a Creative Person

Creative Power that Comes from Imagination

Japanese title: *Sozoteki Ningen no Himitsu*
Lecture given on August 27, 2011,
at Sohonzan Nasu Shoja of Happy Science,
Tochigi Prefecture, Japan

- Chapter Two -

Power Up Your Intellectual Strength

The Art of Reading to Triumph in Life

Japanese title: *Chiteki Tairyoku Zokyo Ho*
Lecture given on August 26, 2010,
at Chiba Shoshinkan of Happy Science,
Chiba Prefecture, Japan

- Chapter Three -

The Power of Perseverance

Mindset and Strategies to Keep Succeeding

Japanese title: *Nintairyoku*
Lecture given on August 24, 2017,
at the Special Lecture Hall of Happy Science, Japan

ABOUT THE AUTHOR

RYUHO OKAWA was born on July 7th 1956, in Tokushima, Japan. After graduating from the University of Tokyo with a law degree, he joined a Tokyo-based trading house. While working at its New York headquarters, he studied international finance at the Graduate Center of the City University of New York. In 1981, he attained Great Enlightenment and became aware that he is El Cantare with a mission to bring salvation to all humankind. In 1986, he established Happy Science. It now has members in over 160 countries across the world, with more than 700 local branches and temples as well as 10,000 missionary houses around the world. The total number of lectures has exceeded 3,300 (of which more than 150 are in English) and over 2,850 books (of which more than 600 are Spiritual Interview Series) have been published, many of which are translated into 37 languages. Many of the books, including *The Laws of the Sun* have become best sellers or million sellers. To date, Happy Science has produced 23 movies. The original story and original concept were given by the Executive Producer Ryuho Okawa. Recent movie titles are *Beautiful Lure–A Modern Tale of "Painted Skin"* (live-action, May 2021), *Into the Dreams…and Horror Experiences* (live-action, August 2021), and *The Laws of the Universe–The Age of Elohim* (animation movie, October 2021). He has also composed the lyrics and music of over 450 songs, such as theme songs and featured songs of movies. Moreover, he is the Founder of Happy Science University and Happy Science Academy (Junior and Senior High School), Founder and President of the Happiness Realization Party, Founder and Honorary Headmaster of Happy Science Institute of Government and Management, Founder of IRH Press Co., Ltd., and the Chairperson of NEW STAR PRODUCTION Co., Ltd. and ARI Production Co., Ltd.

WHAT IS EL CANTARE?

El Cantare means "the Light of the Earth," and is the Supreme God of the Earth who has been guiding humankind since the beginning of Genesis. He is whom Jesus called Father and Muhammad called Allah, and is the Creator in Shintoism, *Ame-no-Mioya-Gami*. Different parts of El Cantare's core consciousness have descended to Earth in the past, once as Alpha and another as Elohim. His branch spirits, such as Shakyamuni Buddha and Hermes, have descended to Earth many times and helped to flourish many civilizations. To unite various religions and to integrate various fields of study in order to build a new civilization on Earth, a part of the core consciousness has descended to Earth as Master Ryuho Okawa.

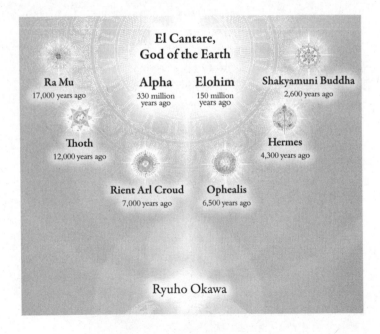

**El Cantare,
God of the Earth**

Ra Mu
17,000 years ago

Alpha
330 million
years ago

Elohim
150 million
years ago

Shakyamuni Buddha
2,600 years ago

Thoth
12,000 years ago

Hermes
4,300 years ago

Rient Arl Croud
7,000 years ago

Ophealis
6,500 years ago

Ryuho Okawa

Alpha is a part of the core consciousness of El Cantare who descended to Earth around 330 million years ago. Alpha preached Earth's Truths to harmonize and unify Earth-born humans and space people who came from other planets.

Elohim is a part of El Cantare's core consciousness who descended to Earth around 150 million years ago. He gave wisdom, mainly on the differences of light and darkness, good and evil.

Shakyamuni Buddha was born as a prince into the Shakya Clan in India around 2,600 years ago. When he was 29 years old, he renounced the world and sought enlightenment. He later attained Great Enlightenment and founded Buddhism.

Hermes is one of the 12 Olympian gods in Greek mythology, but the spiritual Truth is that he taught the teachings of love and progress around 4,300 years ago that became the origin of the current Western civilization. He is a hero that truly existed.

Ophealis was born in Greece around 6,500 years ago and was the leader who took an expedition to as far as Egypt. He is the God of miracles, prosperity, and arts, and is known as Osiris in the Egyptian mythology.

Rient Arl Croud was born as a king of the ancient Incan Empire around 7,000 years ago and taught about the mysteries of the mind. In the heavenly world, he is responsible for the interactions that take place between various planets.

Thoth was an almighty leader who built the golden age of the Atlantic civilization around 12,000 years ago. In the Egyptian mythology, he is known as god Thoth.

Ra Mu was a leader who built the golden age of the civilization of Mu around 17,000 years ago. As a religious leader and a politician, he ruled by uniting religion and politics.

WHAT IS A SPIRITUAL MESSAGE?

We are all spiritual beings living on this earth. The following is the mechanism behind Ryuho Okawa's spiritual messages.

1 You are a spirit

People are born into this world to gain wisdom through various experiences and return to the other world when their lives end. We are all spirits and repeat this cycle in order to refine our souls.

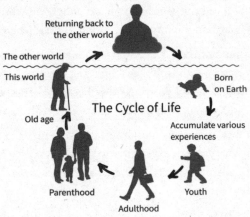

2 You have a guardian spirit

Guardian spirits are those who protect the people living on this earth. Each of us has a guardian spirit that watches over us and guides us from the other world. They are one of our past lives, and are identical in how we think.

3 How spiritual messages work

Since a guardian spirit thinks at the same subconscious level as the person living on earth, Ryuho Okawa can summon the spirit and find out what the person on earth is actually thinking. If the person has already returned to the other world, the spirit can give messages to the people living on earth through Ryuho Okawa.

1 The guardian spirit / spirit in the other world...

2 Goes inside Ryuho Okawa in this world

3 Okawa speaks the words of the guardian spirit / spirit

The spiritual messages of more than 1,200 sessions have been openly recorded by Ryuho Okawa since 2009, and the majority of these have been published. Spiritual messages from the guardian spirits of living politicians such as U.S. President Trump, former Japanese Prime Minister Shinzo Abe and Chinese President Xi Jinping, as well as spiritual messages sent from the Spirit World by Jesus Christ, Muhammad, Thomas Edison, Mother Teresa, Steve Jobs and Nelson Mandela are just a tiny pack of spiritual messages that were published so far.

Domestically, in Japan, these spiritual messages are being read by a wide range of politicians and mass media, and the high-level contents of these books are delivering an impact even more on politics, news and public opinion. In recent years, there have been spiritual messages recorded in English, and English translations are being done on the spiritual messages given in Japanese. These have been published overseas, one after another, and have started to shake the world.

For more about spiritual messages and a complete list of books, visit okawabooks.com

ABOUT HAPPY SCIENCE

Happy Science is a global movement that empowers individuals to find purpose and spiritual happiness and to share that happiness with their families, societies, and the world. With more than 12 million members around the world, Happy Science aims to increase awareness of spiritual truths and expand our capacity for love, compassion, and joy so that together we can create the kind of world we all wish to live in.

Activities at Happy Science are based on the Principles of Happiness (Love, Wisdom, Self-Reflection, and Progress). These principles embrace worldwide philosophies and beliefs, transcending boundaries of culture and religions.

Love teaches us to give ourselves freely without expecting anything in return; it encompasses giving, nurturing, and forgiving.

Wisdom leads us to the insights of spiritual truths, and opens us to the true meaning of life and the will of God (the universe, the highest power, Buddha).

Self-Reflection brings a mindful, nonjudgmental lens to our thoughts and actions to help us find our truest selves—the essence of our souls—and deepen our connection to the highest power. It helps us attain a clean and peaceful mind and leads us to the right life path.

Progress emphasizes the positive, dynamic aspects of our spiritual growth—actions we can take to manifest and spread happiness around the world. It's a path that not only expands our soul growth, but also furthers the collective potential of the world we live in.

PROGRAMS AND EVENTS

The doors of Happy Science are open to all. We offer a variety of programs and events, including self-exploration and self-growth programs, spiritual seminars, meditation and contemplation sessions, study groups, and book events.

Our programs are designed to:
* Deepen your understanding of your purpose and meaning in life
* Improve your relationships and increase your capacity to love unconditionally
* Attain peace of mind, decrease anxiety and stress, and feel positive
* Gain deeper insights and a broader perspective on the world
* Learn how to overcome life's challenges
  ... and much more.

*For more information, visit **happy-science.org**.*

CONTACT INFORMATION

Happy Science is a worldwide organization with faith centers around the globe. For a comprehensive list of centers, visit the worldwide directory at *happy-science.org*. The following are some of the many Happy Science locations:

UNITED STATES AND CANADA

New York
79 Franklin St., New York, NY 10013
Phone: 212-343-7972
Fax: 212-343-7973
Email: ny@happy-science.org
Website: happyscience-usa.org

New Jersey
725 River Rd, #102B, Edgewater, NJ 07020
Phone: 201-313-0127
Fax: 201-313-0120
Email: nj@happy-science.org
Website: happyscience-usa.org

Florida
5208 8th St., Zephyrhills, FL 33542
Phone: 813-715-0000
Fax: 813-715-0010
Email: florida@happy-science.org
Website: happyscience-usa.org

Atlanta
1874 Piedmont Ave., NE Suite 360-C
Atlanta, GA 30324
Phone: 404-892-7770
Email: atlanta@happy-science.org
Website: happyscience-usa.org

San Francisco
525 Clinton St.
Redwood City, CA 94062
Phone & Fax: 650-363-2777
Email: sf@happy-science.org
Website: happyscience-usa.org

Los Angeles
1590 E. Del Mar Blvd., Pasadena, CA 91106
Phone: 626-395-7775
Fax: 626-395-7776
Email: la@happy-science.org
Website: happyscience-usa.org

Orange County
10231 Slater Ave., #204
Fountain Valley, CA 92708
Phone: 714-659-1501
Email: oc@happy-science.org
Website: happyscience-usa.org

San Diego
7841 Balboa Ave., Suite #202
San Diego, CA 92111
Phone: 626-395-7775
Fax: 626-395-7776
E-mail: sandiego@happy-science.org
Website: happyscience-usa.org

Hawaii
Phone: 808-591-9772
Fax: 808-591-9776
Email: hi@happy-science.org
Website: happyscience-usa.org

Kauai
3343 Kanakolu Street, Suite 5
Lihue, HI 96766, U.S.A.
Phone: 808-822-7007
Fax: 808-822-6007
Email: kauai-hi@happy-science.org
Website: happyscience-usa.org

Toronto

845 The Queensway
Etobicoke ON M8Z 1N6 Canada
Phone: 1-416-901-3747
Email: toronto@happy-science.org
Website: happy-science.ca

Vancouver

#201-2607 East 49th Avenue
Vancouver, BC, V5S 1J9, Canada
Phone: 1-604-437-7735
Fax: 1-604-437-7764
Email: vancouver@happy-science.org
Website: happy-science.ca

INTERNATIONAL

Tokyo

1-6-7 Togoshi, Shinagawa
Tokyo, 142-0041 Japan
Phone: 81-3-6384-5770
Fax: 81-3-6384-5776
Email: tokyo@happy-science.org
Website: happy-science.org

Seoul

74, Sadang-ro 27-gil,
Dongjak-gu, Seoul, Korea
Phone: 82-2-3478-8777
Fax: 82-2-3478-9777
Email: korea@happy-science.org
Website: happyscience-korea.org

London

3 Margaret St.
London,W1W 8RE United Kingdom
Phone: 44-20-7323-9255
Fax: 44-20-7323-9344
Email: eu@happy-science.org
Website: happyscience-uk.org

Taipei

No. 89, Lane 155, Dunhua N. Road
Songshan District, Taipei City 105,
Taiwan
Phone: 886-2-2719-9377
Fax: 886-2-2719-5570
Email: taiwan@happy-science.org
Website: happyscience-tw.org

Sydney

516 Pacific Hwy, Lane Cove North,
NSW 2066, Australia
Phone: 61-2-9411-2877
Fax: 61-2-9411-2822
Email: sydney@happy-science.org

Malaysia

No 22A, Block 2, Jalil Link Jalan Jalil
Jaya 2, Bukit Jalil 57000, Kuala Lumpur,
Malaysia
Phone: 60-3-8998-7877
Fax: 60-3-8998-7977
Email: malaysia@happy-science.org
Website: happyscience.org.my

Brazil Headquarters

Rua. Domingos de Morais 1154,
Vila Mariana, Sao Paulo SP
CEP 04010-100, Brazil
Phone: 55-11-5088-3800
Email: sp@happy-science.org
Website: happyscience.com.br

Nepal

Kathmandu Metropolitan City Ward
No. 15,
Ring Road, Kimdol,
Sitapaila Kathmandu, Nepal
Phone: 97-714-272931
Email: nepal@happy-science.org

Jundiai

Rua Congo, 447, Jd. Bonfiglioli
Jundiai-CEP, 13207-340
Phone: 55-11-4587-5952
Email: jundiai@happy-science.org

Uganda

Plot 877 Rubaga Road, Kampala
P.O. Box 34130, Kampala, Uganda
Phone: 256-79-4682-121
Email: uganda@happy-science.org
Website: happyscience-uganda.org

ABOUT HAPPINESS REALIZATION PARTY

The Happiness Realization Party (HRP) was founded in May 2009 by Master Ryuho Okawa as part of the Happy Science Group to offer concrete and proactive solutions to the current issues such as military threats from North Korea and China and the long-term economic recession. HRP aims to implement drastic reforms of the Japanese government, thereby bringing peace and prosperity to Japan. To accomplish this, HRP proposes two key policies:

1) Strengthening the national security and the Japan-U.S. alliance, which plays a vital role in the stability of Asia.

2) Improving the Japanese economy by implementing drastic tax cuts, taking monetary easing measures and creating new major industries.

HRP advocates that Japan should offer a model of a religious nation that allows diverse values and beliefs to coexist, and that contributes to global peace.

*For more information, visit **en.hr-party.jp***

HAPPY SCIENCE ACADEMY
JUNIOR AND SENIOR HIGH SCHOOL

Happy Science Academy Junior and Senior High School is a boarding school founded with the goal of educating the future leaders of the world who can have a big vision, persevere, and take on new challenges.

Currently, there are two campuses in Japan; the Nasu Main Campus in Tochigi Prefecture, founded in 2010, and the Kansai Campus in Shiga Prefecture, founded in 2013.

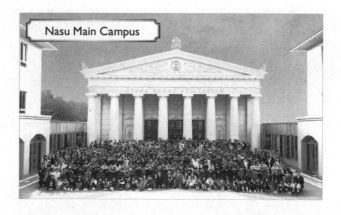

Nasu Main Campus

Kansai Campus

HAPPY SCIENCE UNIVERSITY

THE FOUNDING SPIRIT AND THE GOAL OF EDUCATION

Based on the founding philosophy of the university, "Exploration of happiness and the creation of a new civilization," education, research and studies will be provided to help students acquire deep understanding grounded in religious belief and advanced expertise with the objectives of producing "great talents of virtue" who can contribute in a broad-ranging way to serve Japan and the international society.

FACULTIES

Faculty of human happiness

Students in this faculty will pursue liberal arts from various perspectives with a multidisciplinary approach, explore and envision an ideal state of human beings and society.

Faculty of successful management

This faculty aims to realize successful management that helps organizations to create value and wealth for society and to contribute to the happiness and the development of management and employees as well as society as a whole.

Faculty of future creation

Students in this faculty study subjects such as political science, journalism, performing arts and artistic expression, and explore and present new political and cultural models based on truth, goodness and beauty.

Faculty of future industry

This faculty aims to nurture engineers who can resolve various issues facing modern civilization from a technological standpoint and contribute to the creation of new industries of the future.

ABOUT IRH PRESS USA

IRH Press USA Inc. was founded in 2013 as an affiliated firm of IRH Press Co., Ltd. Based in New York, the press publishes books in various categories including spirituality, religion, and self-improvement and publishes books by Ryuho Okawa, the author of over 100 million books sold worldwide. For more information, visit *okawabooks.com*.

Follow us on:

Facebook: Okawa Books **Twitter:** Okawa Books
Goodreads: Ryuho Okawa **Instagram:** OkawaBooks
Pinterest: Okawa Books

——— **NEWSLETTER** ———

To receive book related news, promotions and events, please subscribe to our newsletter below.

https://okawabooks.us11.list-manage.com/subscribe?u=1fc70960eefd92668052ab7f8&id=2fbd8150ef

——— **MEDIA** ———

OKAWA BOOK CLUB

A conversation about Ryuho Okawa's titles, topics ranging from self-help, current affairs, spirituality and religions.

Available at iTunes, Spotify and Amazon Music.

Apple iTunes:
https://podcasts.apple.com/us/podcast/okawa-book-club/id1527893043

Spotify:
https://open.spotify.com/show/09mpgX2iJ6stVm4eBRdo2b

Amazon Music:
https://music.amazon.com/podcasts/7b759f24-ff72-4523-bfee-24f48294998f/Okawa-Book-Club

BOOKS BY RYUHO OKAWA

RYUHO OKAWA'S LAWS SERIES

The Laws Series is an annual volume of books that are mainly comprised of Ryuho Okawa's lectures on various topics that highlight principles and guidelines for the activities of Happy Science every year. *The Laws of the Sun*, the first publication of the laws series, ranked in the annual best-selling list in Japan in 1987. Since then, all of the laws series' titles have ranked in the annual best-selling list for more than two decades, setting socio-cultural trends in Japan and around the world.

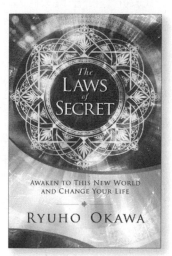

The 27th Laws Series

THE LAWS OF SECRET

AWAKEN TO THIS NEW WORLD
AND CHANGE YOUR LIFE

Paperback • 248 pages • $16.95
ISBN: 978-1-942125-81-5

Our physical world coexists with the multi-dimensional spirit world and we are constantly interacting with some kind of spiritual energy, whether positive or negative, without consciously realizing it. This book reveals how our lives are affected by invisible influences, including the spiritual reasons behind influenza, the novel coronavirus infection, and other illnesses.

The new view of the world in this book will inspire you to change your life in a better direction, and to become someone who can give hope and courage to others in this age of confusion.

THE TRILOGY

The first three volumes of the Laws Series, *The Laws of the Sun*, *The Golden Laws*, and *The Nine Dimensions* make a trilogy that completes the basic framework of the teachings of God's Truths. *The Laws of the Sun* discusses the structure of God's Laws, *The Golden Laws* expounds on the doctrine of time, and *The Nine Dimensions* reveals the nature of space.

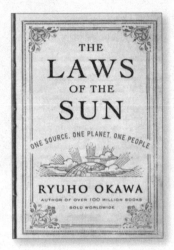

THE LAWS OF THE SUN

ONE SOURCE, ONE PLANET, ONE PEOPLE

Paperback • 288 pages • $15.95
ISBN: 978-1-942125-43-3

IMAGINE IF YOU COULD ASK GOD why He created this world and what spiritual laws He used to shape us—and everything around us. If we could understand His designs and intentions, we could discover what our goals in life should be and whether our actions move us closer to those goals or farther away.

At a young age, a spiritual calling prompted Ryuho Okawa to outline what he innately understood to be universal truths for all humankind. In *The Laws of the Sun*, Okawa outlines these laws of the universe and provides a road map for living one's life with greater purpose and meaning.

In this powerful book, Ryuho Okawa reveals the transcendent nature of consciousness and the secrets of our multidimensional universe and our place in it. By understanding the different stages of love and following the Buddhist Eightfold Path, he believes we can speed up our eternal process of development. *The Laws of the Sun* shows the way to realize true happiness—a happiness that continues from this world through the other.

---

*For a complete list of books, visit **okawabooks.com***

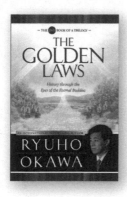

THE GOLDEN LAWS
HISTORY THROUGH THE EYES OF THE ETERNAL BUDDHA

Paperback • 201 pages • $14.95
ISBN: 978-1-941779-81-1

Throughout history, Great Guiding Spirits of Light have been present on Earth in both the East and the West at crucial points in human history to further our spiritual development. *The Golden Laws* reveals how Divine Plan has been unfolding on Earth, and outlines 5,000 years of the secret history of humankind. Once we understand the true course of history, through past, present and into the future, we cannot help but become aware of the significance of our spiritual mission in the present age.

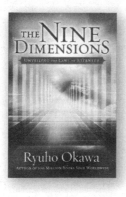

THE NINE DIMENSIONS
UNVEILING THE LAWS OF ETERNITY

Paperback • 168 pages • $15.95
ISBN: 978-0-982698-56-3

This book is a window into the mind of our loving God, who designed this world and the vast, wondrous world of our afterlife as a school with many levels through which our souls learn and grow. When the religions and cultures of the world discover the truth of their common spiritual origin, they will be inspired to accept their differences, come together under faith in God, and build an era of harmony and peaceful progress on Earth.

*For a complete list of books, visit **okawabooks.com***

LAWS SERIES

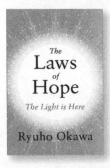

THE LAWS OF HOPE
THE LIGHT IS HERE

Paperback • 224 pages • $16.95
ISBN:978-1-942125-76-1

This book provides ways to bring light and hope to ourselves through our own efforts, even in the midst of sufferings and adversities. Inspired by a wish to bring happiness, success, and hope to humanity, Okawa shows us how to look at and think about our lives and circumstances. By making efforts in your current circumstances, you can fulfill your mission to shed light on yourself and those around you.

THE LAWS OF HAPPINESS
LOVE, WISDOM, SELF-REFLECTION AND PROGRESS

Paperback • 264 pages • $16.95
ISBN: 978-1-942125-70-9

What is happiness? In this book, Ryuho Okawa explains that happiness is not found outside us; it's found within us, in how we think, how we look at our lives in this world, what we believe in, and how we devote our hearts to the work we do. Even as we go through suffering and unfavorable circumstances, we can always shift our mindset and become happier by simply *giving love* instead of *taking love*.

THE LAWS OF SUCCESS
A SPIRITUAL GUIDE TO TURNING YOUR HOPES INTO REALITY

Paperback • 208 pages • $15.95
ISBN: 978-1-942125-15-0

The Laws of Success offers 8 spiritual principles that, when put to practice in our day-to-day life, will help us attain lasting success. The timeless wisdom and practical steps that Ryuho Okawa offers will guide us through any difficulties and problems we may face in life, and serve as guiding principles for living a positive, constructive, and meaningful life.

*For a complete list of books, visit **okawabooks.com***

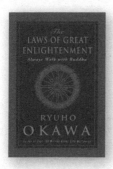

THE LAWS OF GREAT ENLIGHTENMENT
ALWAYS WALK WITH BUDDHA

Paperback • 232 pages • $17.95
ISBN: 978-1-942125-62-4

Constant self-blame for mistakes, setbacks, or failures and feelings of unforgivingness toward others are hard to overcome. Through the power of enlightenment we can learn to forgive ourselves and others, overcome life's problems, and courageously create a brighter future ourselves. The Laws of Great Enlightenment addresses the core problems of life that people often struggle with and offers advice on how to overcome them based on spiritual truths.

THE LAWS OF PERSEVERANCE
REVERSING YOUR COMMON SENSE

Paperback • 268 pages • $14.95
ISBN: 978-1-937673-56-7

"No matter how much you suffer, the Truth will gradually shine forth as you continue to endure hardships. Therefore, simply strengthen your mind and keep making constant efforts in times of endurance, however ordinary they may be. "

-From Postscript

THE LAWS OF WISDOM
SHINE YOUR DIAMOND WITHIN

Paperback • 268 pages • $14.95
ISBN: 978-1-941779-36-1

This book guides you along the path on how to acquire wisdom, so that you can break through any wall you are facing or will confront in your life or in your business. By reading this book, you will be able to avoid getting lost in the flood of information and go beyond the level of just amassing knowledge. You will be able to come up with many great ideas, make effective planning and strategy and develop your leadership while receiving good inspiration.

---

*For a complete list of books, visit **okawabooks.com***

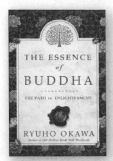

THE ESSENCE OF BUDDHA
THE PATH TO ENLIGHTENMENT

Paperback • 208 pages • $14.95
ISBN: 978-1-942125-06-8

In this book, Ryuho Okawa imparts in simple and accessible language his wisdom about the essence of Shakyamuni Buddha's philosophy of life and enlightenment—teachings that have been inspiring people all over the world for over 2,500 years. By offering a new perspective on core Buddhist thoughts, Okawa brings these teachings to life for modern people. This book distills a way of life that anyone can practice to achieve a life of self-growth, compassionate living, and true happiness.

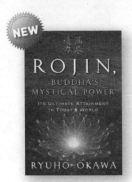

ROJIN, BUDDHA'S MYSTICAL POWER
ITS ULTIMATE ATTAINMENT IN TODAY'S WORLD

Paperback • 224 pages • $16.95
ISBN: 978-1-942125-82-2

In this book, Ryuho Okawa has redefined the traditional Buddhist term *Rojin* and explained that in modern society it means the following: the ability for individuals with great spiritual powers to live in the world as people with common sense while using their abilities to the optimal level. This book will unravel the mystery of the mind and lead you to the path to enlightenment.

THE TRUE EIGHTFOLD PATH
GUIDEPOSTS FOR SELF-INNOVATION

Paperback • 256 pages • $16.95
ISBN: 978-1-942125-80-8

This book explains how we can apply the Eightfold Path, one of the main pillars of Shakyamuni Buddha's teachings, as everyday guideposts in the modern-age to achieve self-innovation to live better and make positive changes in these uncertain times.

For a complete list of books, visit **_okawabooks.com_**

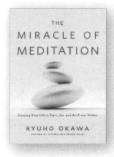

THE MIRACLE OF MEDITATION

OPENING YOUR LIFE TO PEACE, JOY, AND THE POWER WITHIN

Paperback • 207 pages • $15.95
ISBN: 978-1-942125-09-9

This book introduces various types of meditation, including calming meditation, purposeful meditation, reading meditation, reflective meditation, and meditation to communicate with heaven. Through reading and practicing meditation in this book, we can experience the miracle of meditation, which is to start living a life of peace, happiness, and success.

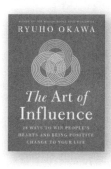

THE ART OF INFLUENCE

28 WAYS TO WIN PEOPLE'S HEARTS AND BRING POSITIVE CHANGE TO YOUR LIFE

Paperback • 264 pages • $15.95
ISBN: 978-1-942125-48-8

Ryuho Okawa offers 28 questions he received from people who are aspiring to achieve greater success in life. At times of trouble, setback, or stress, these pages will offer you the inspirations you need at that very moment and open a new avenue for greater success in life. The practiced wisdom that Okawa offers in this book will enrich and fill your heart with motivation, inspiration, and encouragement.

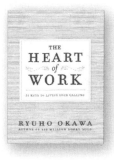

THE HEART OF WORK

10 KEYS TO LIVING YOUR CALLING

Paperback • 176 pages • $12.95
ISBN: 978-1-942125-03-7

In this book, Ryuho Okawa shares 10 key philosophies and goals to live by to guide us through our work lives and triumphantly live our calling. There are key principles that will help you get to the heart of work, manage your time well, prioritize your work, live with long health and vitality, achieve growth, and more.

*For a complete list of books, visit **okawabooks.com***

THE POWER OF BASICS
Introduction to Modern Zen Life of Calm, Spirituality and Success

THE CHALLENGE OF THE MIND
An Essential Guide to Buddha's Teachings:
Zen, Karma, and Enlightenment

TWICEBORN
My Early Thoughts that Revealed My True Mission

THE STRONG MIND
The Art of Building the Inner Strength
to Overcome Life's Difficulties

THE ROYAL ROAD OF LIFE
Beginning Your Path of Inner Peace, Virtue, and a Life of Purpose

WORRY-FREE LIVING
Let Go of Stress and Live in Peace and Happiness

THE HELL YOU NEVER KNEW
and How to Avoid Going There

THE REAL EXORCIST
Attain Wisdom to Conquer Evil

HEALING FROM WITHIN
Life-Changing Keys to Calm, Spiritual, and Healthy Living

---

*For a complete list of books, visit **okawabooks.com***

MUSIC BY RYUHO OKAWA

THE THUNDER

a composition for repelling the Coronavirus

We have been granted this music from our Lord. It will repel away the novel Coronavirus originated in China. Experience this magnificent powerful music.

Search on YouTube

the thunder coronavirus 🔍   for a short ad!

THE EXORCISM

prayer music for repelling Lost Spirits

Feel the divine vibrations of this Japanese and Western exorcising symphony to banish all evil possessions you suffer from and to purify your space!

Search on YouTube

the exorcism repelling 🔍

for a short ad!

 Listen online
Spotify iTunes Amazon